Deck Building Easy for Beginners

Step By Step Guide on How to Make Your Own Deck for Use All Year Round

Introduction

Are you thinking about building a deck to make your outdoor space more functional —for things like hosting barbecues, extra sitting space, outdoor play area, and more)?

Would you like to increase your home's appeal, value, and more but don't know how to do it yourself without making potentially dangerous mistakes when building a deck?

Are you looking for a blueprint that takes away the guesswork from everything to do with building a deck broken down using simple, straightforward language that will ensure you have all your questions answered by the time you complete reading?

If you have answered YES, keep reading...

This book will provide the direction you need to design and build a DIY deck without spending a fortune!

Decks are an important part of our homes. If you go to a home with a deck and one without, you will notice a clear difference. In addition to feeling 'complete,' the home with a deck will feel more valuable, which shall give you more bargaining power if you ever decide to sell your home since the square footage will have increased, and so will the house's general value.

Wanting a deck for your home is not everything. It is also in your best interest to build a professional and outstanding deck because you don't want to be spending your deck-enjoyment time fixing the deck or worrying about it breaking down soon or not being useful when the weather changes.

Naturally:

As someone who wants to embark on a DIY deck project, you probably have all manner of questions going through your mind:

- *Where do I start?*
- *Which deck type is best for my home and my all-year-round needs?*
- *What do I need to build such a deck – how do I decide which material is best for my needs and situation?*
- *How do I ensure the deck continues to be useful for the long haul?*
- *How do I ensure the structure is safe for use?*

If you have these and other similar questions, rest assured that the book in your hands will answer all your deck-building questions in simple language!

Here is a sneak peek of some of the topics covered in this book;

- Compelling reasons why you should strive to build a deck
- The different types of decks you can build
- What to know before you start building your deck, mistakes to avoid, and safety precautions to take
- Basic parts of a deck – A discussion of basic parts of every deck
- Deck building tools
- How to make different types of decks
- Deck repair and maintenance
- **And much more!**

Creating an all-year-round deck is challenging; no one can dispute that. However, the step-by-step guidance in this book will help you realize that you do not need to spend a lot of money creating that outdoor space you have always wanted.

This book will teach you everything you need to know to make your deck, including how to incorporate your deck vision and ideas with all-weather comfort to suit all your needs!

Let us begin.

PS: I'd like your feedback. If you are happy with this book, please leave a review on Amazon.

Please leave a review for this book on Amazon by visiting the page below:

https://amzn.to/2VMR5qr

Table of Contents

Introduction 2

Chapter 1: Benefits of Having a Deck _____ 10

Chapter 2: Things to Note About Deck Building _____ 14

    Deck Styles _____ 21

    Factor in Decking Patterns _____ 25

    Know More About Your Area Building Codes ____ 35

    Maintain All Safety Precautions _____ 36

Chapter 3: Basic Parts of a Deck _____ 38

    Decks Boards/Decking _____ 38

    Footing _____ 39

    Post and Post Anchors _____ 44

    Deck Beams _____ 45

    Joists and Rim Joists _____ 46

    Deck Blocking _____ 47

Deck Railing _____ 47

Balusters and Balustrade _____ 48

Stairway _____ 49

Chapter 4: Deck Building Tools _____ 51

Chapter 5: Deck Building: Projects _____ 64

Deck 1: A Herringbone Inlayed Deck _____ 65

Deck 2: Diagonal Decking Pattern _____ 80

Deck 3: Composite Decking with a Floating Deck   105

Deck 4: A Trex Deck Transformation _____ 136

Deck 5: Backyard Full Deck Project _____ 184

Deck 6: A Curved Deck with Millboard Products _ 239

Deck 7: A Floating Deck on A Sloping Yard _____ 263

Deck 8: A Two-Level Pool Deck _____ 285

Deck 9: Front Yard Deck _____ 356

Deck 10: A Deck Around the Pool _____ 388

Chapter 6: Deck Maintenance and Repair __ 422

Conclusion _____ **431**

Chapter 1: Benefits of Having a Deck

Deck building is becoming one of the most popular homeowner projects, which, although attributable to many things, is because a DIY deck is easy to customize based on taste, preference, and even budget.

For example, you can decide to make a deck that is an addition to your family room, dining, or bedroom. You can also go wild and build a spacious 'outdoor' deck that will be enough for more than one activity and that can host many people!

But as with any DIY project, it is essential to understand the main components of deck construction because deck-building is a systematic process. Following these steps one after each other, as this guide will instruct, will prove that deck building can be easy and fun!

I initially desired to have a deck for outdoor planting and relaxing purposes, but when a friend told me that I could spice my deck even further, it got me thinking,

"What more advantages does a deck have?"

Decks Add More Value to The House

I am not asking you to build a deck so you can sell your house, but comparing a house with a deck and one without, the house with a deck has more value!

Let me prove it with a few statistics:

Think of this – You build a deck for around US$13,000, or thereabout, while the house is worth around US$150,000, the house would total to US$163,000, right? With this amount, let us now determine how much this house will appreciate each year if the house is well maintained.

Black Knight reported that the national appreciation rate is roughly 3.8 percent yearly[1]. With our figure of US$163,000, if this house is yours, you can smile knowing that you will enjoy a profit of roughly US$6,194 or more annually! Not bad, right, because it is better than what you would have if your house had no deck?

Please remember that the figures above are from a layman's perspective. We can get a more factual idea by looking at the following statistic.

---

[1] https://www.ownerly.com/real-estate/average-home-appreciation/

A study done by NAR/NALP [2] reports that a deck made of wood will help you recover around 106 percent of its value once you sell the house. Thus, if you use around US$9,450 to build a deck, the estimated amount it will bring in once you sell the house will be around US$10,000.

As you can see, adding that small or big deck will truly boost your bargaining power if you ever decide to sell your home.

A Deck Gives You More Room

We all want to maximize our spaces and do the things we love, like outdoor gardening, painting, outdoor catering, etc. You will have more room to do all that, depending on which deck you build.

Before I had a deck, I had a huge desire to expand my love for plants and flowers from indoors to outdoors. After I built my deck, I can manage to do exactly that, and now my deck is surrounded by beautiful lavenders, begonias, coleus, and caladiums!

---

[2] https://dr04a97154x4n.cloudfront.net/does-deck-increase-value-your-home.html

Decks are Relatively Inexpensive

As you will discover in this guide, a DIY deck will cost roughly half or slightly more than hiring a deck contractor. You may argue that the only difference between hiring a deck builder and building it yourself is labor, but that is not entirely true. You may not get the right quotation for the materials, which may be doubled or tripled without your consent!

Besides the labor and materials, a contractor may charge you differently based on design, which may further drive up the cost.

Are you convinced that deck building will be a God-sent addition to your home and life? Good.

Next, let us set a few things straight to help you understand deck building better before we get to building.

Chapter 2: Things to Note About Deck Building

As it is with building anything, you need good planning and decision-making to build an ideal deck. With this said, you should know a few things:

Determine Where the Deck Will Be

Most decks are at the front part of the house, but the truth is that you can have a deck in many places, such as;

Over a room

As an extension of your master bedroom

At the side of your house

Detached from the house, among others.

We will discuss this more in subsequent chapters.

Create a budget

There are several things to note when thinking about budget. The first is that it is essential to know that the national average for building a standard deck is around US$12,600[3]. However, this is a mere estimate because lumber and other deck building prices are not stagnant, and prices might fluctuate.

Better homes and gardens[4] give an estimate of how much you will use for different deck sizes:

---

[3] https://www.fixr.com/costs/build-deck
[4] https://bit.ly/3pJSH1G

- For an 8x8 foot raised deck built with treated lumber, the cost will be about US$1,300

- For an 8x8 foot raised deck built with red cedar, the total cost will be about US$2,000

- A 12 feet by 16 feet raised deck built by 12 feet by 16 feet treated lumber raised deck that has stairs will cost around US$3,100 in materials

- 16x16 foot raised deck built using composite decking materials will cost around US$5,600 minimum to US$9,800

Please note that the actual prices may vary. In addition, if you add extra features such as planters, built-in benches, or shade structures, be prepared to add to the total cost per square foot.

Be More Open to Different Deck Materials

There are many decking materials; thus, do not settle for wood if you have not yet known about other materials. Other decking materials include;

Pressure-treated woods

These types of woods have some preservatives that make the wood weather-resistant. These woods include cedar, pine, and redwood

Premium hardwoods

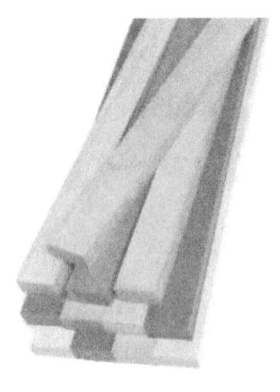

These woods are known for their durability. They include Ipe, teak, and more Brazilian wood species.

Composite decking materials

These woods have recycled plastic and wood fibers. These types of materials are easy to maintain. However, they are more expensive to purchase than normal wood

Plastic planks or PVC

These materials are the best for harsh weather because they do not rot easily. Although these materials are good for harsh weather, they are quite expensive.

Aluminum decking materials

Many prefer this type of decking because of its material. Aluminum is firm enough such that even when it rains, you will not fall due to it becoming slippery. This decking material is also very costly.

Consider Your Deck's Style

Before you get right to building your deck, think about style. Your deck should complement rather than compete with the house's design.

Let us say you want to build a deck that has a curve design with cared railings. This design may look beautiful before you build it, but after building it, you may realize that it does not look as you initially thought. The trick, therefore, is to follow your house's proportions, lines, and overall architecture. Doing this will make the deck so seamless and natural that no one will tell that the deck was an addition.

Let us look at some of the most common deck styles to help you understand why it is essential to factor this in before you start building the deck.

Deck Styles

The Classic Flow

This design mostly uses wood. It has a natural look, making it the most popular choice if you want a deck that perfectly blends in with your yard.

The Craftsman

This deck is also wood-made (you can also use various materials) but has a more traditional look. This deck has simple lines and does not have any additions, decorations, or embellishments.

Besides what we have discussed, this decking has a characteristically low roofline and wide eaves. These two factors help the deck space remain safe from elements such as rain and sun.

The farmhouse

This style is simple and characterized by wide flooring and railings. Most of the decks made from this style use wood or composite materials. Those with a deck made from this style have said it is easy to maintain, meaning you do not have to worry about too much upkeep.

The Mid Century Modern

This design is relatively new but gaining popularity because it has a minimalist theme. So, if you want to give your house a minimal, modern look, this is the deck design to build!

Homeowners who have made their decks from this design say these decks do well with materials such as composite or wood. You can use this design to build split-level decks, a-frame decks, and multi-level decks.

The Scandinavian

This is your ideal design if you want a deck with a floor with as minimal straight uniform lines as possible! Besides having minimal lines, this design is quite simple to build!

The best material for this type of design is untreated wood. Untreated wood is the best because it turns a rich and beautiful silver-grey color over time. This deck has a beautiful look that is easy to maintain.

Factor in Decking Patterns

Can you notice something unique from the different designs we have just discussed? The flooring patterns are different, right? Before you build your deck, decide which pattern works for you!

There are several types of patterns. They include:

The chevron and herringbone pattern

This pattern brings out that visual effect and adds interest and texture to the deck. Creating these two patterns asks you to alternate your boards in opposite directions.

The diagonal pattern

This pattern will give your deck that special look –it will look like your deck space has some curves. To do this deck, you will install the boards at a 45-degree angle across the joists (these are lumber or wood-made horizontal structures that run between beams).

The diamond pattern

As the name suggests, this pattern has a diamond shape. As you can see from the image above, it has straight lines and diagonal lines. Many love this pattern because its shape strengthens the deck floor since the woods are nailed or screwed in from different angles.

The horizontal pattern

Like diagonal decking patterns, this pattern demands you nail or screw the boards in a straight line. Many love this pattern because of its contemporary feel and look, and it is quite cheap to build. Because they are easy to build, you will not need to do a lot of maintenance.

The Parallel Pattern

A parallel pattern is your best choice if you want your deck attached to your house. This pattern is difficult to build as the decks share a common card pool built separately, but if done well, your deck will have a unique synergy that many will ogle!

The parquet or basketweave pattern

This decking pattern is characterized by small squares, making the deck have a uniquely elegant look. Those who have made decks using this pattern say the decks can withstand harsh weather elements better than decks made using other patterns.

The picture frame pattern

If you would like a deck so perfect that it leaves no cut ends of your boards exposed and a deck that can support a lot of weight, then this pattern is for you!

Picture framing means you will install a border deck board around the outside part of the deck, as seen in the picture above. This pattern has a board running over the outside rim joist, which was then flush with the upper part of the deck, something that covers the end grain of your deck boards.

The pinstripe pattern

If you want a deck floor that blends classic and modern, then the pinstripe pattern is for you!

To build this deck, you will have two narrow boards with standard boards on each side. Through this pattern, your deck will have that enhanced look that many decks lack.

The tile pattern

Tile decks are attractive, efficient, and economical decks that are perfect for you if you are looking for an easy-to-maintain deck. We all know that tiles come in different colors; thus, it is easy to get the exact color that matches your interior décor!

Know More About Your Area Building Codes

Before building my deck, I was not all that concerned about permits. I always wondered:

"Why do I need a permit for something as common as a deck?"

Well, a permit will ensure that you comply with all set regulations. Additionally, a permit will push you to build a structurally fit deck that will prevent any injuries from deck collapses and other deck-related damages.

And what rules should you be familiar with before building your deck?

The 30" rule

There is a written –and sometimes unwritten– rule requiring you to have a permit before building a deck higher than 30 inches off the ground. If you build a deck that is below 30 inches, you will not need a permit as that is considered a porch deck.

Foundationally:

I cannot give the exact permits you need to start building because they vary from state to state. The best advice I can give you is to consult your local government.

Generally, the following are some of the most common steps you will have to go through;

- Contact your city's building inspections department
- After contacting the said department, you will receive instructions on what documents to have to apply for the permit
- After filling in the documents, submit them along with two copies of your construction plans and a site plan

Maintain All Safety Precautions

Before, during, and after building your deck, do major housekeeping. This means you should carefully store and handle all tools such as lumber, nails, screws, and hammers.

Store the tools you are not using aside and carefully clean your tools, then store them carefully after use. In addition, wear the right gear while building. That means wearing hard hats, reflectors, gloves, safety boots, goggles, and other safety gear.

You might also be in a hurry to start and finish your deck. Although this may be a good idea, be self-aware, especially of workplace stress. Do not lift weights you cannot handle, work long hours, and engage in risky working conditions such as drinking alcohol while working.

Mind your posture and your back as you work because working when lifting or sitting may lead to sprains, strains, overexertion, dislocation, or muscle tears. Mind your posture because a bad posture increases the chances of injuries.

We are at the right time in this book to discuss another important thing that will be foundational when we begin building different deck projects: *the basic parts of a deck.*

Chapter 3: Basic Parts of a Deck

Decks might have many small components, but all decks have the following parts;

Decks Boards/Decking

The decking is the 'main floor' part of the deck —as shown in the image above. Your decking can be made of different materials such as;

- Wood decking material

- Pressure-treated wood decking material

- Tropical hardwood decking material

- Cedar decking material

- Redwood decking material

- Composite decking material

- Plastic lumber decking material

Footing

A deck footing is the support section that supports the decking. The support sections can be made from poured or cast concrete and go deep below the surface. There are several types of deck footings, such as;

- **Poured concrete footings** – these are done by digging a hole, putting a deck post in the hole, then finally pouring in concrete.

- **Building post footings** – these are made by digging a hole, then putting in a pressure-treated wood that extends above the ground, adding cement footing, and finally backfilling the post

- **Precast stackable cement footings** - These footing types are dropped into place without mixing or pouring anything. You will first dig a hole, put a precast base in, and then stack each piece on top. For anchoring, you will attach a threaded anchor rod to the pieces and extend them up through the center of the stack.

- **Deck blocks** – these are cement blocks cast before setting them up. Once they are ready, you will bury them slightly below the ground surface.

Deck Building Made Easy for Beginners

- **Screw/helical piles** – these are manufactured steel footings that screw down into the ground. You will need some hydraulic machinery for the installation process; many people love them because they need no digging.

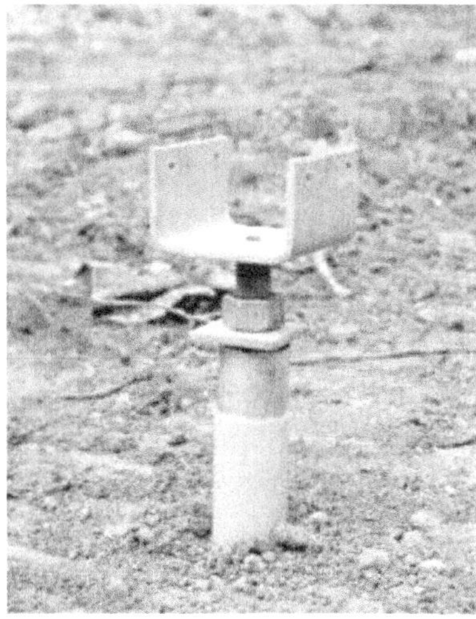

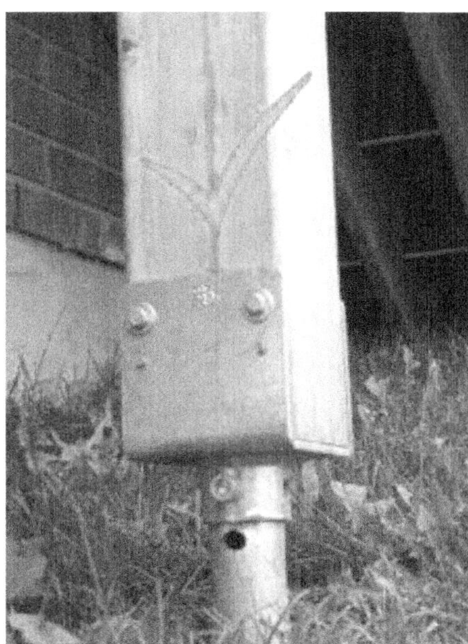

Deck Building Made Easy for Beginners

Post and Post Anchors

As you can tell from the image above, post and post anchors are vertically placed boards that you will attach to the footings through post anchors.

On the other hand, post anchors, also called concrete piers, are support structures that help hold the beams from the ground level. They also help boost airflow underneath the deck, making it easy to maintain the space under the deck.

Deck Beams

Beams rest on top of your posts horizontally. Beams will frame out your deck size while also boosting structural support to all parts that lay atop them, such as deck boards and joists.

Joists and Rim Joists

A decking joist is a board you will use as a structural base for your deck frame. There is a big difference between decking and joists, and it is essential to note it: Joists will run perpendicular to the house, and decking will be parallel to the house.

Deck Blocking

Deck blocking is a technique that attaches the wooden blocks to the joists. Deck blocking helps increase the rail attachment and joist strength. Also, deck blockings help make the deck more solid.

Deck Railing

Deck railing consists of guardrails, an umbrella term for varying parts such as railing caps, balusters, posts, and rails. Deck rails provide structure to the deck and offer more practical uses such as giving a place for you to leash the dog, among others

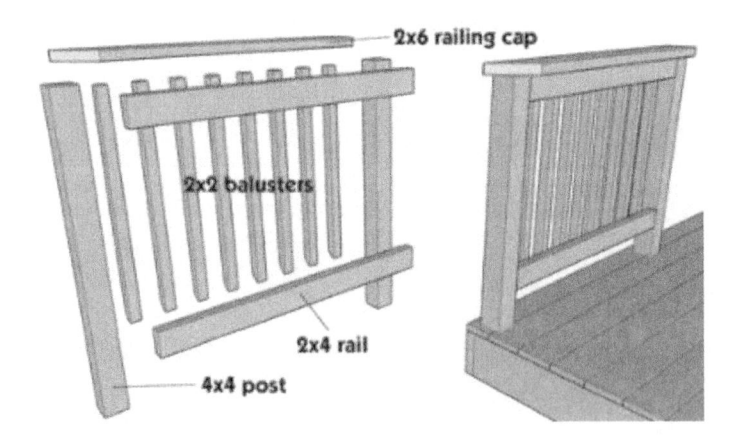

Balusters and Balustrade

Balusters are vertical legs or posts; they look like vases placed on railings. Balusters help strengthen the railings and add beauty to the whole deck.

Baluster   Balusters   Balustrade

Stairway

This structure will help you –and others– get up to the deck –the stairs come in here. There is no set rule on how your stairway should look because you can choose from the many available styles.

When we get to the deck projects section of this book, you may notice other deck parts not mentioned in this section. Don't let that scare you because different decks can have different parts.

The parts mentioned here are what you can expect to find on every deck, irrespective of its design or size.

Next, let us get our tools ready:

Chapter 4: Deck Building Tools

The most foundational tools you will need when building a deck include:

Saw

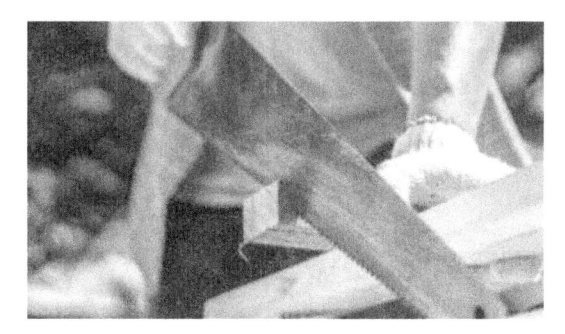

A saw will be one of your most important tools because you will need it to cut your boards to size. To make cleaner cuts, I recommend using the circular saw. Also, the circular saw will speed up the cutting process, thus saving time. Also, keep your hand saw close because it will also come in handy when doing detailed cuts.

Chalk line

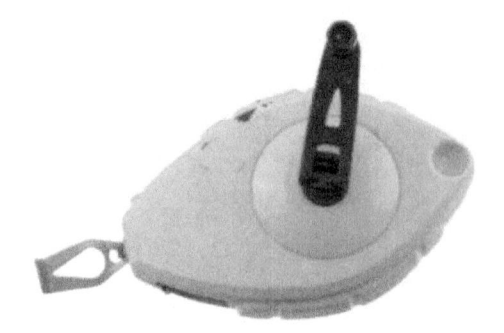

Since you will be doing a lot of measuring, the chalk line will help you mark marking cutting points. You can also use your chalk lines to make lines, which will help ensure that you saw the wood in a straight line.

Tape measure

Your chalk will come in very handy when making cutting marks. However, to have the deck board fit perfectly, you need a tape measure, so always remember to get the correct measurements and mark your cutting points correctly with your chalk pen.

Carpenter's level

Imagine measuring your wood, cutting, and building your deck only to find that it is not as even as it should be! That would be frustrating because you will have to disassemble the whole project; it might also be costly, especially if you have to measure and cut your wood all over again.

To avoid all these problems, get yourself a carpenter's level.

Power drill

You will need screws and nails to attach the boards. To attach them, you will need a drill.

The trick with drills is to know which type of wood you are working with. For example, when working with hardwoods such as Ipe, you will need a drill because you will need to pre-drill all the holes.

I recommend drilling instead of nailing because it makes decks stronger.

BoWrench Deck Straightening Tool

A BoWrench is an essential tool for wooden decks because the chances are high that some boards will not fit in as straight as possible. So, when you screw in a board and notice that it is taking a lot of elbow grease and you have no extra help, get yourself a BoWrenching Decking tool.

A BoWrench is a self-locking deck board bender that will help you save time and energy while ensuring you make a professional deck.

Shovels

You cannot avoid digging when it comes to deck building: you will need it when clearing foundation space and building your footing. Get yourself a shovel with a narrow blade – this is good for digging shallow post holes.

Pipe and Squeeze Clamps

A pipe clamp allows you to attach an object –in this case, wood– firmly while you work on the said wood.

Decking screws

I recommend using screws for decking instead of nails. This is because screws will hold down the deck more securely, which is essential for wrapping prevention. Additionally, screws will be easier to remove than nails when you make mistakes.

Framing hammer

A framing hammer has a textured head designed explicitly for hammering in nails and screws. You can also use this, or another hammer called the 'finishing hammer,' to install nails that go through the side of the deck. Finally, get a rubberwood mallet. This hammer is better suited for joists, boards, and posts.

Orbital sander

If you decide to make a wooden deck, you may need to sand your boards before treating them. This technique is essential because it adds treatment, removes, and loses wood fibers and stains, allowing the wood to get the right amount of treatment.

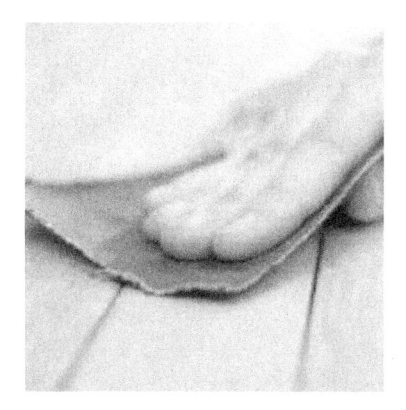

If you do not have an orbital sander, you can use a belt sander or sandpaper.

Assorted hardware

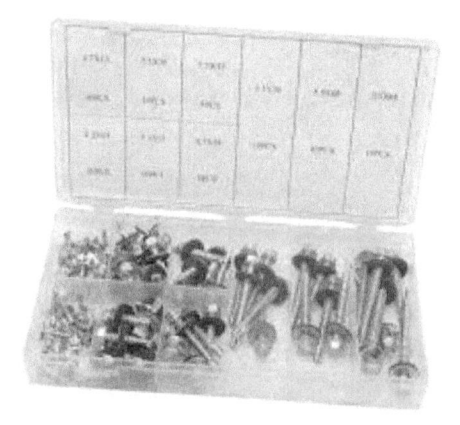

You might need various tiny tools such as nuts, bolts, washers, and tie-backs, but the assorted tools you need will depend on the type of deck you will build. We will learn more about their uses as we focus on our deck projects. For now, you only need to keep them in mind.

With our tools ready, I have one question for you.

"Do you know what type of deck you want?"

If not, let me help you choose in the next chapter.

Chapter 5: Deck Building: Projects

This chapter aims to do two things;

- First, I will show you how to make the different floor patterns we discussed in chapter 2.

- Secondly, I will show you how to build various decks while incorporating different designs and patterns

Deck 1: A Herringbone Inlayed Deck

Materials Required

- Digging materials
- Shovel
- Sica fence post mix
- Cement
- Wood/lumber
- Saw
- String
- Tape measure
- Bolts

- Anchors

Procedure

- First, clear the space. For this specific project, we had to go further and uproot a tree

- Next, add your posts

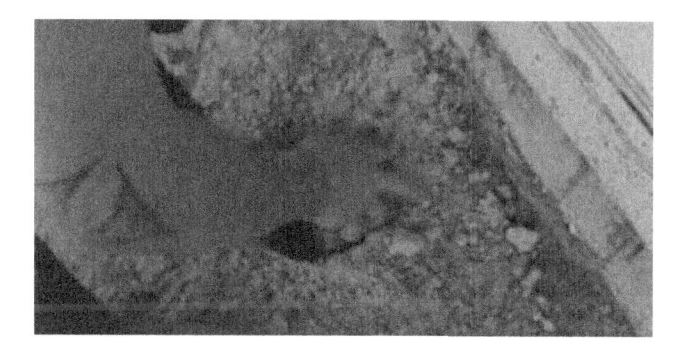

- Remember to have concrete in the post holes before you put in the posts. I used a Sica fence post mix and cement as a topping agent to ensure that the post remained firmly in place.

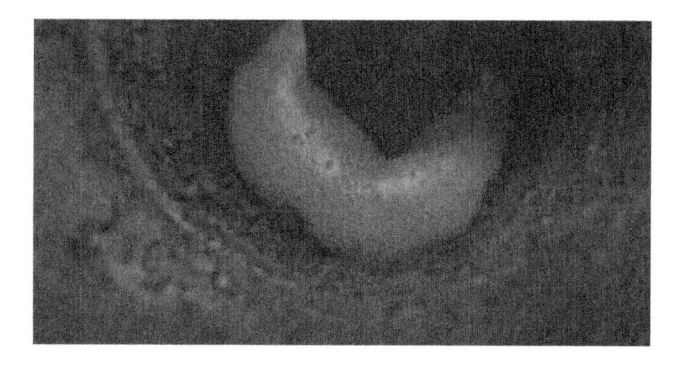

The post holes are 24 inches deep.

- After doing all the posts, tie a string from one end to the other to affirm that they are all at a leveled height.

- Take a tape measure and affirm that the space between the edge of the property and where the posts are is equal. Measure all posts.

The space between one post and another should also be the same.

Next, let us make our joists. To do this;

- First, mark and cut the wood according to your preferred measurements.

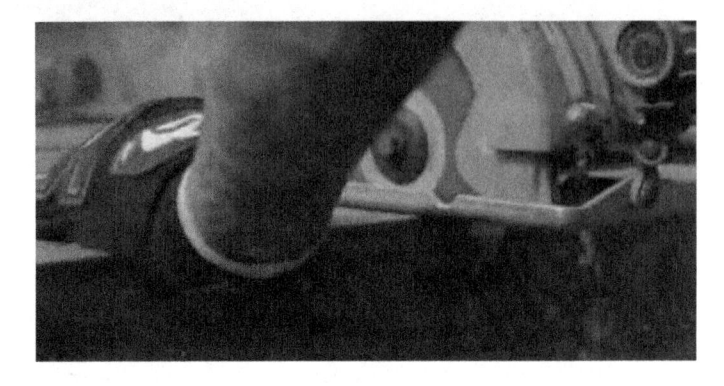

As you continue measuring and cutting your lumber, keep in mind the entire shape of your joist. Below was what I was thinking of the whole time.

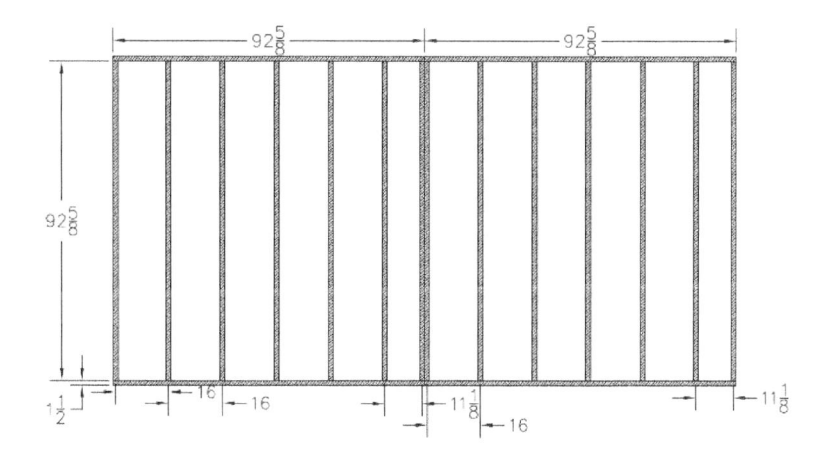

- Next, screw the boards together.

- After screwing in one board to another, use your level to ensure they are not slanted.

You should have this:

You can do your joists as you wish. I made mine in sections.

- Remember to support your joist edges. If you do not have anchors, as I had for this project, use the deck blocking technique discussed in chapter 3.

While you bolt, do big bolts on all major corners to help make the deck stronger.

Let us go to the next step. We are making the herringbone pattern. We mentioned that you alternate your boards in opposite directions to make this pattern.

For the screws, I will be using camo screws.

- When screwing the board, you will drive up the screw through the side of the board through the joists underneath. After doing this, look at the board – you will find it hard to see the screw!

- After cutting the boards to ones with a slanted end to create that diagonal look, start anywhere you like. I start with one big board at the center and then fill the pattern using it as guidance.

For the edges, you can start from one end to the other because the boards will have the same height.

Next, let us make the stairs

To do this;

- First, screw in straight pieces of timber to the deck.

- Then, on top of these pieces of wood, add some wood pieces at the end to help you know where the step will be.

- After knowing exactly where the stair would reach, close it up by adding a board around it.

- Finally, add boards on top to cover the skeleton.

Your final project should resemble something close to the image below:

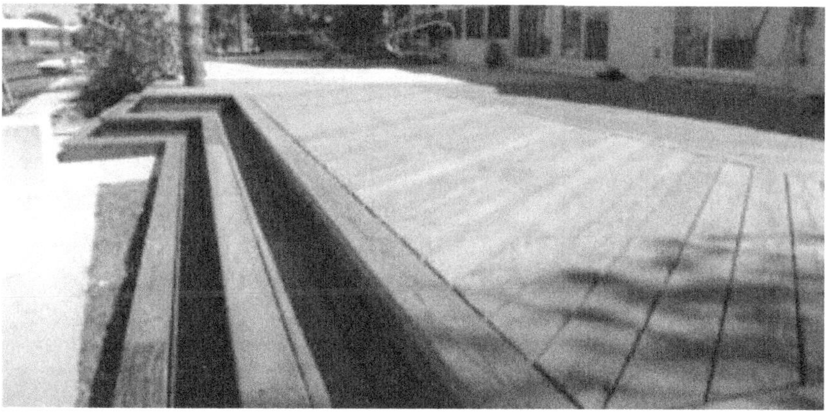

Deck 2: Diagonal Decking Pattern

Materials Required

- Hammer

- Tape Measure

- String

- Iron Rods

- Sawn tanalised lumber

- Carpenter's level

- Chalk or pencil

- Galvanized screws

- Drill
- Screws
- Anchors
- Ruler
- Crow Bar
- Spacers
- Kreg decking system

Procedure

- First, use your hammer, tape measure, iron rods, and string to mark out the full area of where the deck will be.

- Next, lay some pad foundations.

Do this by diffing small holes. I did holes measuring 300mm square by 300mm deep.

Next, mix up wet concrete and pour it into the holes till full.

Keep in mind that the pad foundations need to be 1 meter apart.

Next, build and fit the deck's subframe.

- Take your lumber – I used 4by2 inch sawn tanalised timber– and make clearance holes 400mm apart along the lumber beam.

- Next, set the height of the frame and mark it.

- Next, use a masonry drill bit and hammer action drill to drill through the clearance holes.

- Next, apply a wall plug and hammer it in tightly.

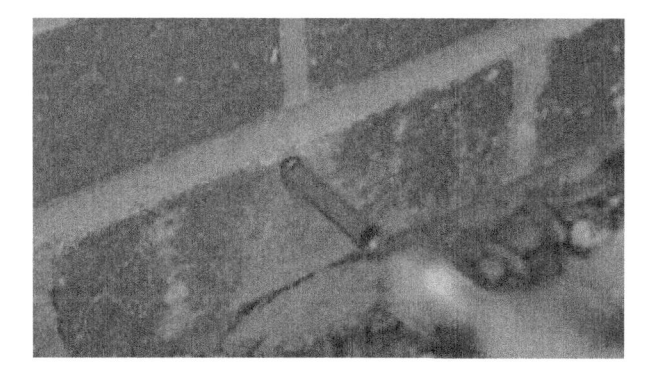

Next, drive in your bolts through the clearance holes you made earlier.

- Next, drive it through the brickwork. Drive the bolts through the beam to bite tightly into the wall plugs.

- Next, mark and lay the places you will put your joists hangers.

Next, screw the joists in using galvanized screws.

Next, mark and cut all the joists to the required length.

- Next, lay the cut lumber across the deck area.

- Next, fix another beam on the front section.

- Next, fix the straight beams to the anchors.

- Next, cut some noggins and fix them between the joists to stop them from twisting.

- Next, take a crowbar, put some wooden chocks under the beam and lift the frame until it is level. To confirm it is level, use a carpenter's level.

- Next, fix some timber offcuts to the side of the joists and directly over the pad foundations to help reinforce the joist to take any weight.

- Next, apply a wood treatment to the lumber.

- Next, construct the deck's subframe. To do this, trim the back corner of the lumber. Set an angle and place a straight length of lumber across the top of the joists, then mark using a pencil.

- Next, trim back the lumber with a hand saw.

Deck Building Made Easy for Beginners

- Next, add another beam to the cut angled edge of the joists.

Page | 95

- Next, take one of the decking beams, clamp it, and screw it to the front of the bearing beam. This will act as the fascia board.

- Next, apply the top decking planks. Ensure all joints sit directly on the joists below.

- Next, measure and cut the next piece of plank using a circular saw

- Next, add a spacer and put them in between the planks.

- Next, use a Kreg decking system to drill screws diagonally.

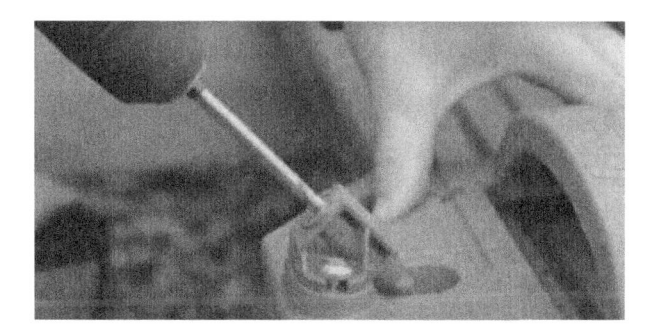

Remember to screw down all your planks on the edges into the joists below to hold them firmly in position.

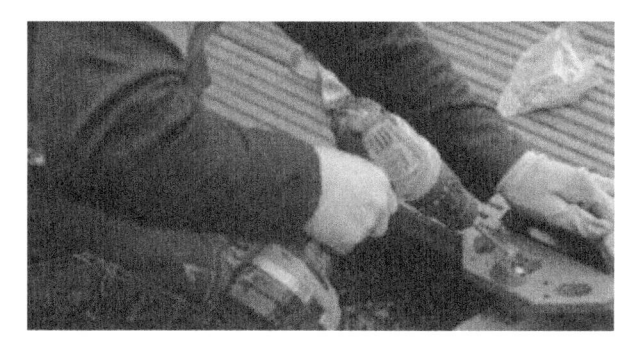

- If some obstacles are in the deck's way, say pipes on the wall, take a pencil and draw around them

- Next, clamp down the section you have marked to a stable workbench and cut around it with a jig saw. Then fix it back.

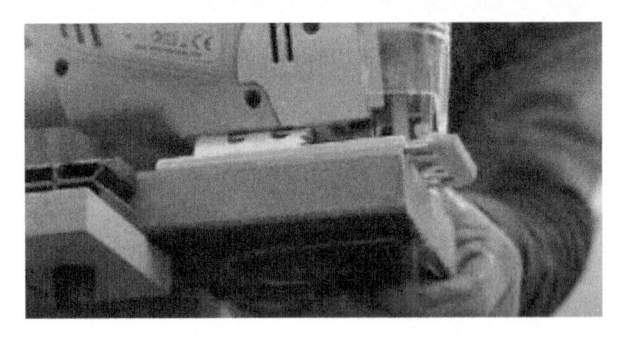

Continue laying and fixing down the decking planks. Leave an overhang at the corner where you will create an angle.

- Next, run a string line across the corner where you are about to cut.

- Now make a line following the string and cut across the line.

Finally, fix the rest of the planks until you complete the whole deck.

- Apply some wood preserver to all the cut edges, and your project is complete.

Deck Building Made Easy for Beginners

Deck 3: Composite Decking with a Floating Deck

Materials Required

- Shovel

- Wheelbarrow

- Skid steer
- Pave base
- Decking blocks
- Tape Measure
- Screws
- Drill bit
- Corner jigs
- Steel butyl tape

Procedure

- First, clear your decking space

Deck Building Made Easy for Beginners

Get a skid steer if the debris proves challenging to remove with a shovel alone.

- Next, make that cleared space as level as possible.

- Now set up some double stakes in each corner to have a layout of where the deck will be.

- Next, dig a trench. This trench will house the deck blocks.

- Next, put a pave base on top of the whole deck area, then add some of the soil you had removed on top of the area you had dug the trenches.

- Next, place the decking blocks on top of the lined soil.

- Now measure the distance from the decking block to the string. Every decking block should sit at that distance.

Also, ensure the distance between the decking blocks is equal.

- Next, set the wood in between the decking block. Use the carpenter's level to ensure everything is level. If unleveled, move the decking block to and for on the dirt until it becomes so.

- Next, use your saw to cut off all the factory ends of all the pressure-treated wood.

- Next, mark and cut the lumber as per your measurements. While cutting, ensure you place it between two supports to prevent pinching.

Deck Building Made Easy for Beginners

Page | 113

Next, screw the lumber boards together. I used the Simpson's strong ties 3" deck drive wood screws for the outside frame.

As you do the screwing, use corner jigs to ensure the wood stays in place. If the woods are not level, you may need to do some lifting by putting some pieces of wood beneath.

- Next, measure and cut your decking boards. You will place these boards on top – they will be the floor of your deck. Start with the inside piece.

Deck Building Made Easy for Beginners

- Next, screw in the anchors for more support.

- Now set the frame on the decking blocks.

When fixing my frame, I noticed the outer frames were not fitting. Only the center frame was fitting in the decking boards.

To address this, I did some deck blocking.

- Next, measure from one corner to the other diagonally and add the rest of the joists.

Deck Building Made Easy for Beginners

- Next, add anchors to those joints – do the screwing diagonally.

- After fixing the anchors, measure once more to affirm you have a square.

- Next, add all the other pieces of wood to complete the deck bunking.

Remember to add the pieces of wood and then the anchors.

This should be your result so far.

- Next, cut more decking boards and small 7-inch pieces of wood.

- Attach these pieces of wood to the planks.

Deck Building Made Easy for Beginners

- Cover that piece up with another plank of wood

Page | 125

- Next, screw it in.

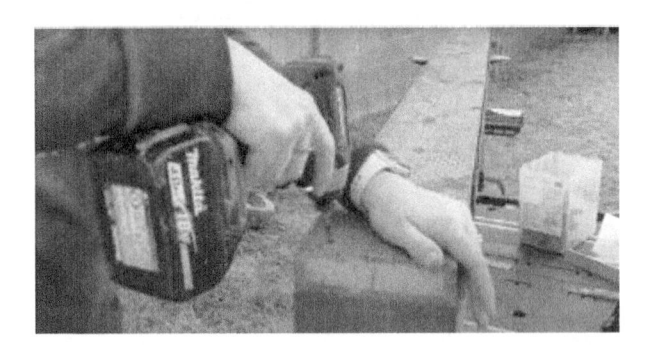

This will be your first step.

- The next step is to attach it to the deck.

- Before installing it, add a weed barrier.

- Put some paver base on top of the barrier to keep it intact.

- Put the step on top of the paver base, then screw it to the deck.

- Put some steel butyl tape on top to ensure the deck lasts longer. This will help divert water when it rains. Also, it will seal all decking holes. It is easy to use; you only need to peel and stick the tape over the joists.

Now we are ready for decking. I will be using Trex decking in rocky harbor color.

- Next, slide the board in.

- On the next row, add another Trex deck and attach the next board.

Page | 129

Deck Building Made Easy for Beginners

- For the last board, use universal clips.

- Next, attach decking to the stair

- Next, attach the board to the stair.

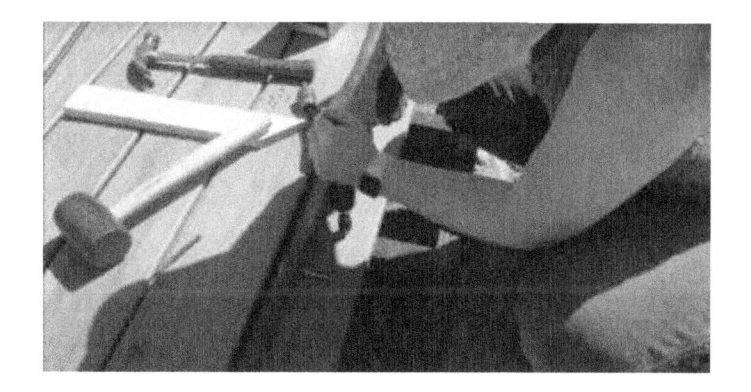

- Finally, saw the edges to clean up the deck edges.

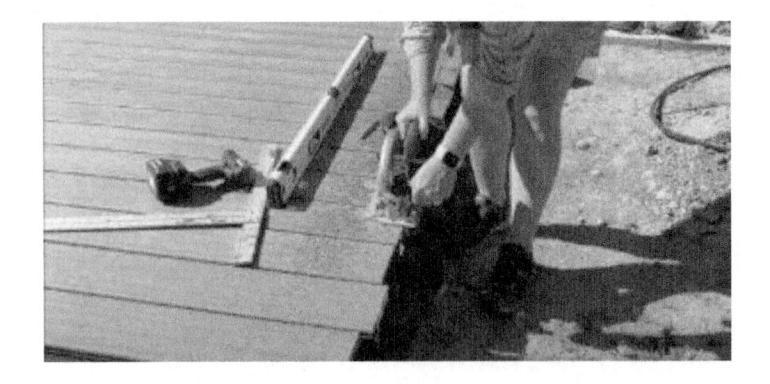

- Finally, finish up by adding a fascia board as a finisher.

- Finally, paint based on your preferences.

And you are done!

Deck 4: A Trex Deck Transformation

This project is ideal for people who have an existing deck and are wondering how to upgrade it easily or attach it to another new deck

Materials Required

- Hammer
- Lumber
- Cable cutter
- Steel cable
- Hurricane clips
- Hydraulic crimping tool
- Concrete mixer
- Shovel

- Cement
- Gravel
- Anchors
- Screws
- Drill bit
- Nails
- Spray
- Sonotube
- Carpenter's level
- Water
- Phillip heads
- Brackets

Procedure

- First, remove the old rotten deck.

Deck Building Made Easy for Beginners

- For old posts that are still safe to use, add some tape to the top to help prevent future rot.

- To finish repairing this old deck, I removed the decking boards and fixed new decking boards.

- The joist hangers were still in good condition for my deck, so I just fixed the decking board.

I wanted to add on a new deck beside the old one. For this new one, I followed the steps below;

- Map out where the deck will be

Use spray paint to mark out the deck area.

- Next, make your post holes.

- Next, pour in some concrete to make the footings

- Do not forget to add Sonotubes into the hole and affirm they are level. To confirm if they are level, use a carpenter's level.

- Next, fill the soil back into the hole. However, remember that you are filling the sides of the tubes to help keep them in place.

- Next, add concrete into the tubes. If you have doubts about mixing the concrete correctly, buy premixed concrete because, with it, you will only need to pour it into your holes and soak it with water.

- Next, vibrate the concrete with rebar.

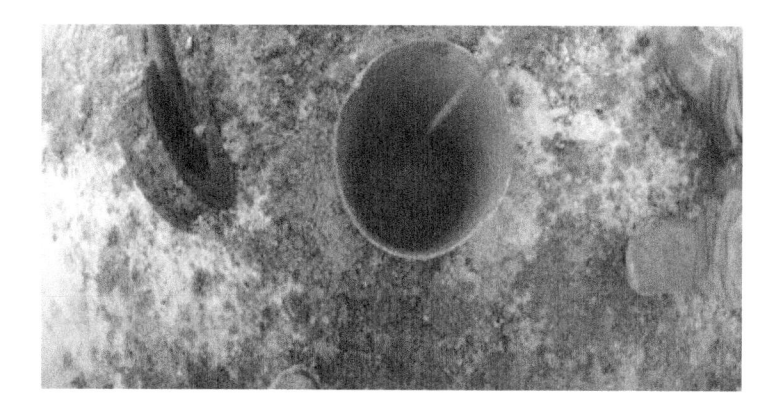

- Next, to allow the concrete to cure, cover it with insulation paper.

- Once the concrete cures, install the poles. To do this, first mark where the post will rest.

- Next, take a hammer drill and create the holes you will use to fix your brackets.

- Now tighten the bolts.

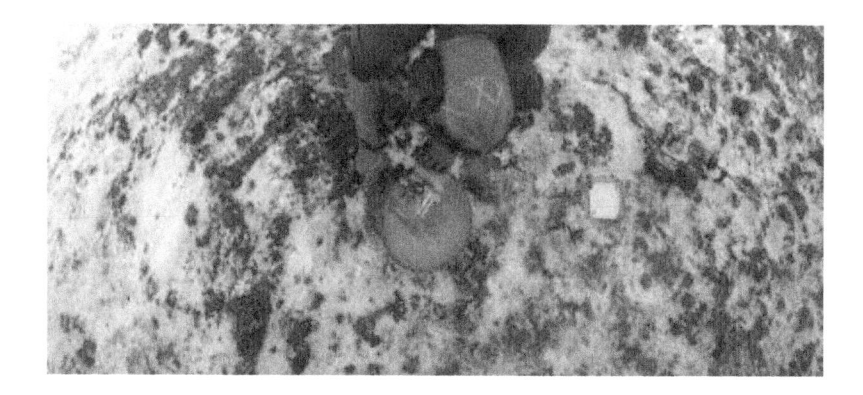

- Hammer in the posts in between the posts.

If you can note from my image, I have more lumber nailed in in a slanted position. This will support the posts.

- Next, screw in the brackets to the posts you have just erected.

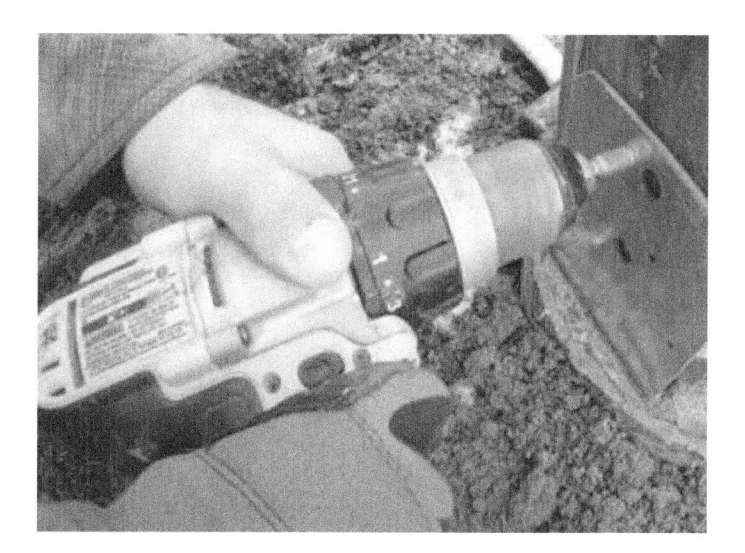

- Next, it is time to fix the joists. Measure your decking height and curve out the notches in which to fix the joist.

- Next, use a Sawzall to finish out the cuts.

Deck Building Made Easy for Beginners

- Now fill the notches with boards.

- Next, affirm the boards are level. Use a carpenter's level.

Deck Building Made Easy for Beginners

- Next, screw the boards to the posts.

- Next, add joist hangers after every 16 inches.

- Now attach the boards to the house wall.

- Next, cut off the excess posts, including removing the support beams.

- Next, fix the corner hangers and fix in the joists

- Add tape atop the posts, then measure and mark every 16 inches. These spots will house the joists. Hurricane clips will hold joists.

- Next, take your lumber, ensure the crown is facing up, then set up the joists.

All you have to do is slide in the lumber.

Deck Building Made Easy for Beginners

- After sliding the joists in, screw all of them into the lumber

- Next, trim the beams' ends using a circular saw.

- Next, install a double joist and joist hangers –this should connect the old and the new deck.

- For a stronger deck, do deck blocking in the middle of the joists, as seen in the image below.

- Next, trim the deck edges.

- Next, measure the outer board length and cover it. This will be your fascia.

- Next, do more deck boarding, but a little bit lower. This will help when putting the deck floor.

- Next, add some Trex to protect the wood and help prevent future rot.

This should be your deck so far.

- The next step is to do Trex decking. I chose rocky harbor and started from the corner, but you can choose one of the many different colors available.

Use a carpenter's pencil to keep the boards at a perfect distance from each other.

And the floor is done

- Next, put the same floor on the old deck. To do this, start by putting some beam tape on the wood.

- Next, adjust and add a few hangers.

- Next, just like we did for the new deck, trim its edges, then add the fascia.

- Next, add on the tape and do the floor.

Page | 171

- Remember that if you have obstacles near the deck –as the picture shows, I have a power station– add some blocking to the ends of the decking

- Next, work on the railings. To do this, first measure where the railing posts will go; I put mine around four feet apart.

- Next, add blocking where the railing posts will go.

- Next, unscrew the last decking boards and re-measure and shape them to fit the railings, as shown below.

- Next, you can add some privacy boards .

- Now take your square tubing, measure them into the railing size you want, then drill them evenly spaced.

- Measure and cut some small plates for use as the bottom plate. Then take your cut metal bars and solder them onto the plate.

- Next, clean your bars. The number of bars you need depends on how big you want your railing to be.

- Next, place the metal bars on your deck

- Next, drill or nail the metal bars to the deck edge.

- After safely securing the metal bars to the deck, it is time to work on the top of the railing. All you will do is to measure, cut, and screw or nail the metal bars to the wood.

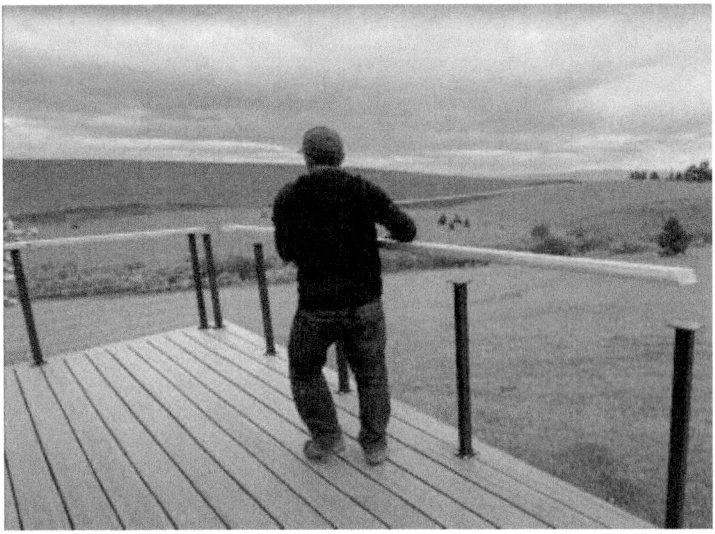

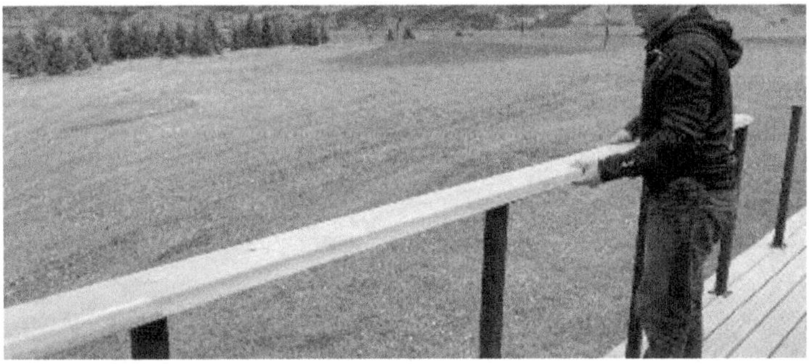

- Next, thread in your stainless-steel cable through the holes of the metal bars.

- Once at the edge, cut the steel cable using a cable cutter, then crimp it using a hydraulic crimping tool.

Do you remember how we built the staircase in deck 1 when building a Herringbone inlay deck? Well, that is what you will do to make your staircase. There really is no particular way to go about building the staircase.

Then, just like we have done with the railings, build the staircase railings the same way

Deck Building Made Easy for Beginners

- Next, place wood on top of the metal bars and attach them together.

- Finally, paste the posts using a dark charcoal solid color stain. This will protect the posts.

For the once-muddy section under the deck, I did some landscaping. And you are done. Congratulations!

Deck Building Made Easy for Beginners

Deck 5: Backyard Full Deck Project

Materials Required

- Hammer

- Brackets

- Raft ties

- Silicone sealant or any other waterproofing tape

- Clamp

- Drill bit

- Circular saw

- Carpenter's chalk

- String

- Wood

- Tape measure

- Power auger

- Carpenter's level

- Pencil

- Nails

Procedure

- First, mark your layout with strings and batter boards.

The trick is to ensure that the batter boards are slightly past the layout. Also, ensure that the strings are level.

- Your layout should also be square. To affirm this, measure diagonally using a tape measure.

- Once all measurements are correct, mark the final spots where the deck will be.

- Next, cut the sod.

- Next, clear the already cut sod.

- With your clear deck layout, mark the spots where the posts will go.

- Next, mark the post positions.

- Next, mark the height of the deck. Your deck should **ALWAYS** be below the door floor height to help with keeping the water out.

- Once you get your height right, post-mark a level line at that height along the house.

- Next, insert the tubes.

- Next, just like we set up posts in the last deck project – deck project 4– do the same here. You will mix your concrete, pour it into the tube, fill in the soil to have the tube stay firm, allow the concrete to cure, fix the brackets, and then fix the posts.

- Remember, if the tube is too high, measure and trim it.

- Also, measure the tube to affirm it is level.

- To ensure the concrete settles well, you can use a shovel or piece of wood to 'press' down the concrete.

- Next, put an anchor bolt inside the concrete to make it plumb.

- Also, do not forget to backfill the fresh concrete, which will help with the curing process.

- After the concrete cures, remove the excess tubing.

- Next, fix in the brackets.

- Next, fit in the posts.

- Next, nail the brackets to the posts.

- After setting up all the posts p, mark the tops using chalk. The line should be level with the height you made on the house.

Deck Building Made Easy for Beginners

- Use the same height measurements to mark the rest of the posts.

- Next, cut the excess height of wood

- Next, attach the deck's support beams. The crown of the beam should always look up. To identify the crown, look at the slight arch on the wood.

- Take two boards, clamp them, and screw or nail them together.

- Next, attach post caps with nails, then set your beams on the post caps.

- Next, apply waterproofing tape to the beams. You can also use silicone sealant.

- Next, do diagonal bracing to help prevent racking.

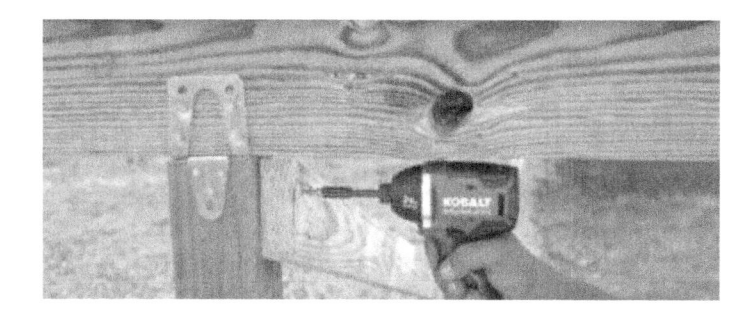

- Next, set up a straight joist against the house at the edge of the deck square.

- Now measure and mark 6 feet from the deck corner, 8 feet from the deck corner, and adjust the joist accordingly,

- The next step is to cut the beams.

- Next, mark the joist floor spacing.

- Next, place each rim joist on a beam and then transfer the lines down the face of each joist, placing an X to the side of the lines –this is where you will attach your joists.

- Next, drill pilot holes right at the end and screw the two boards together.

- Next, secure that corner with a reinforcing bracket.

Deck Building Made Easy for Beginners

- Now position the frame on the beams.

- Next, secure the frame with raft ties.

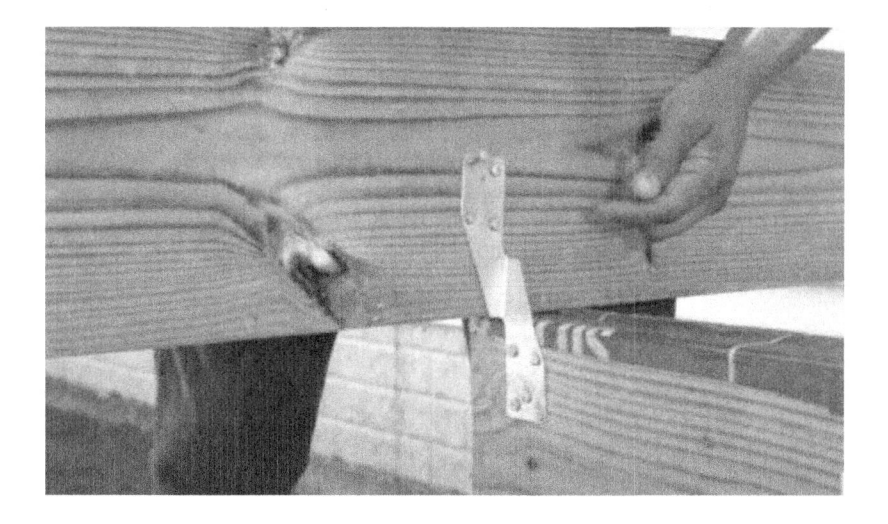

- Next, add bracing to support the parting deck boards.

- Next, install the rest of the beams.

- Next, trim the beams according to the initial measurements.

- Next, attach the finishing beam.

Deck Building Made Easy for Beginners

- Next, support the finishing beam with a bracket.

- Next, install your deck floor.

- Next, mount posts on top of the decking floor. We will begin by the posts by the house, then to the ones on the corners, plus those at the top of the stairs.

For the number of posts, refer to the building laws. To make the posts, follow the steps below;

- First, cut the posts according to your measurements.

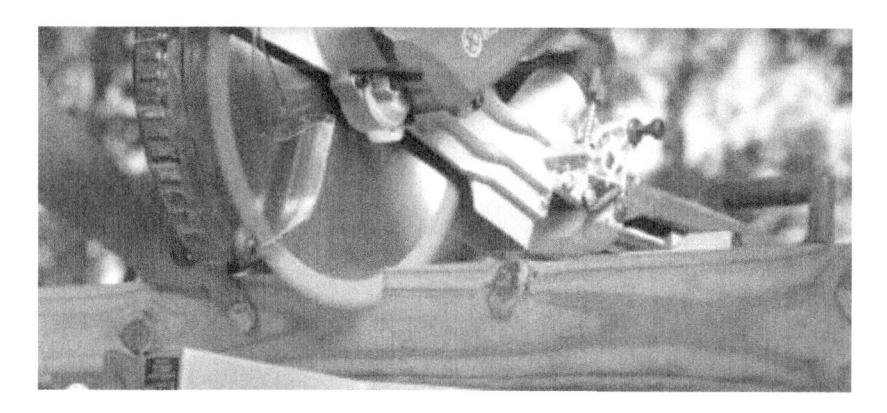

- Whenever you screw in the post, always reinforce it with a bracket.

- After installing all the posts, install parting deck boards next. Do this in the middle of the deck.

- To support these decking boards, add more support decking by the house.

- Next, add in the rest of the decking.

Deck Building Made Easy for Beginners

- Next, trim the edges once the decking boards are laid and screwed down.

Next, work on the railings. To do this, follow the steps below;

- First, add balusters from the bottom. Kindly note that I screwed in mine approximately 4 inches from the bottom

- Next, screw in the top flush

- Next, add in pieces between the baluster space. Space as you desire.

Next, work on the stairs. To do this, remember that they will be 12 equally shaped stringers. These stringers will rest on a solid foundation to avoid unnecessary movement.

Our stairs will have toe kicks or also known as raisers

Finally, our staircase will have railings, and the raisers will be covered.

With this in mind, let us begin.

- First, identify where the bottom step of the staircase will be.

Set a long level on top of the decking; measure the height right where the steps will end. For instance, if the height is

55 inches, you will divide it by 7 (this is the recommended height for staircase steps). Take the result and round it off to the nearest number, and you will get 8; these will be the raisers we will be working towards.

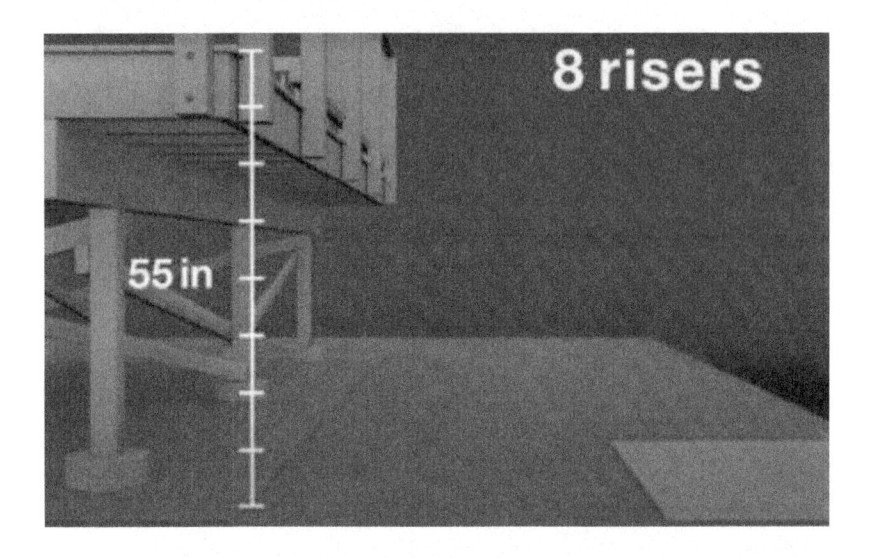

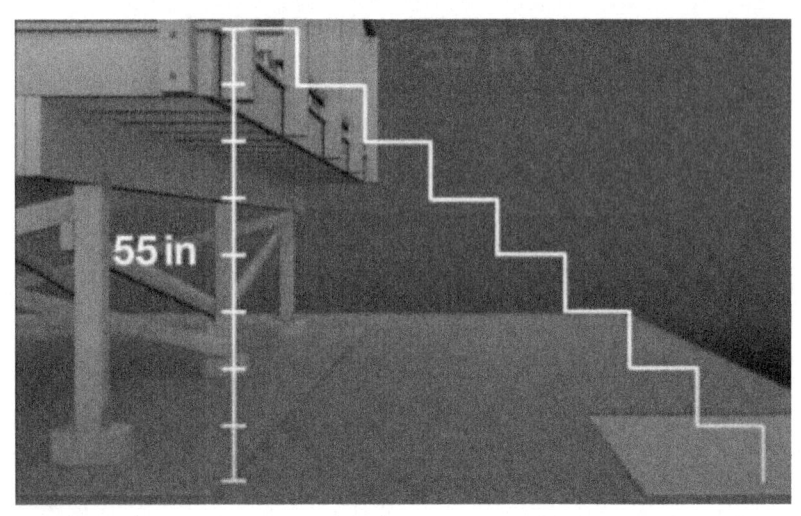

To determine the measurements of each step, divide the original height by the number of raisers. With this in mind, let us get back to building it out.

- Start by building a concrete footer.

- Next, add in the post

- Next, attach a piece of wood, preferably 2x8, to the rim joist to help secure the stringers. Brace it to the beam or joist.

- Next, attach the stringers to the deck.

- Next, attach the stringers to the posts.

- Next, some pads in between the bottom of the staircase

- Next, attach posts from the bottom. As you move up the staircase, secure them with brackets.

- Next, add the toe kicks.

- Next, add the treads.

- Next, clamp the rail board, measure, mark, cut then screw it to the bottom rail.

- Next, use a baluster to locate the top rail.

- Next, screw the top rail to the posts and the deck.

- Next, cut the excess piece of posts

- Next, add a flat piece of wood on top of the rails. This will help anyone hold onto the staircase railing while climbing or coming down.

- Add more raisers to the railing for more stability and surety of its strength.

- You can also add a metal railing to the wood

So far, that is it for the basic work!

For this deck, I added some lighting. To do this, follow the steps below;

- Start by curving out the light spaces.

- Next, mount the light fixtures and covers.

- Next, install and secure a transformer.

- Next, route the cables.

- Next, connect the lights.

- Now install solar.

- For floor lighting, drill the deck floor, then install the light to sit flush.

- Below the deck, do some skirting.

- All you have to do is attach the framing

- You can also close the bottom part of the deck

Deck Building Made Easy for Beginners

And you are done!

Page | 237

Deck Building Made Easy for Beginners

Deck 6: A Curved Deck with Millboard Products

Materials Required

- Carpenter's chalk
- Tape measure
- Saw
- Joist supporters
- Plas Pro 50
- Plas Pro Panhead brackets
- Drill
- Plywood
- Durafix screws

- Sandpaper

Procedure

- Start by building the curved subframe. For this frame, I will not be supporting it with posts off the ground. Instead, I will use a lattice framework. Also, this deck will be a floating deck.

NOTE: You may be wondering, "why a lattice framework?" Well, this framework is better suited for anyone with extra small space. In addition, this framework comes with added strength.

- Mark out the Dura-Lift joist support locations.

- Ensure the spacing is even.

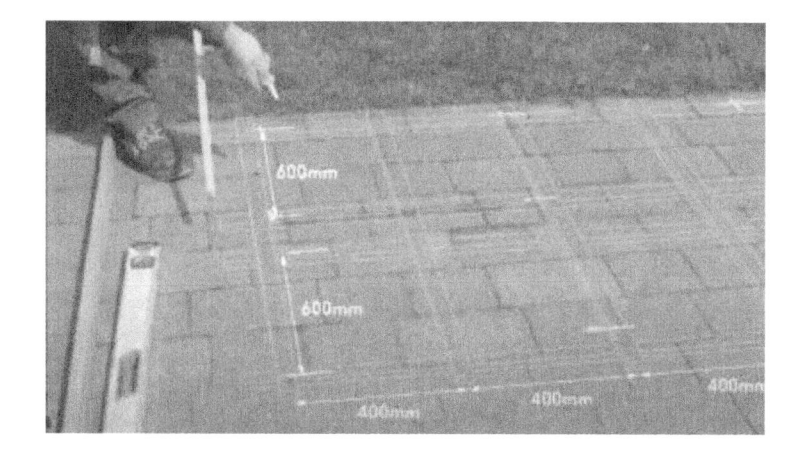

- Next, place the dura-lift joists in the marked positions.

- Turn around the height adjustment ring round the joist cradle – make sure each quarter turn adjusts the height by one millimeter.

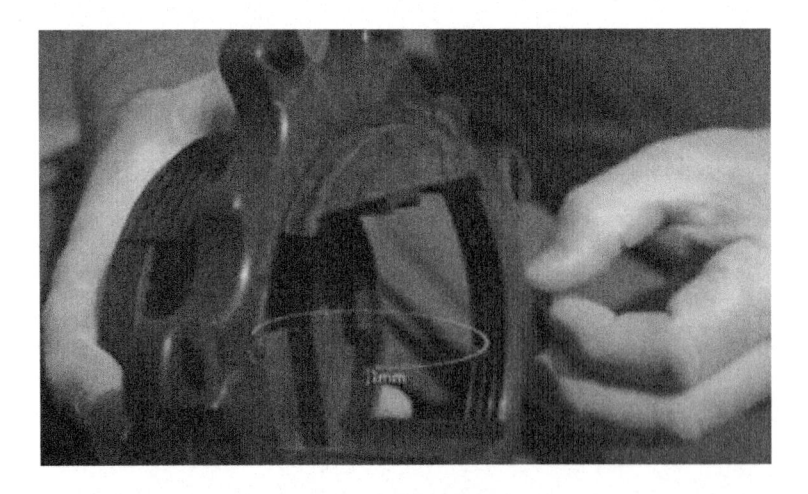

- Next, place Plas Pro 50 50mm into the top of the joist cradles.

- Then adjust the adjusting ring around the joist cradle. This will ensure the joist has fulll support.

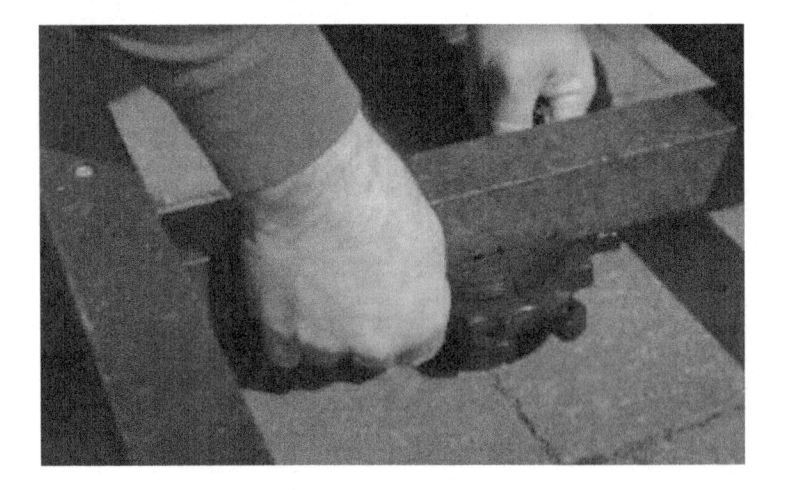

- Next, take locking tabs and insert them into the adjustment ring. Do this on either side.

- Next, add Plas Pro Panhead brackets.

Deck Building Made Easy for Beginners

- Next, drill in the joints. All butt joints must have a 10mm gap to allow ample expansion if temperatures rise.

- Next, set the curve. The trick to doing this right is using a piece of batten or plywood to ensure the line is the same.

- Find the center mark of the radius.

- You will notice that a pencil will not work – it does not show up well. Instead, use a millboard Durafix screw. Just screw it into your moveable plywood.

- This will help create a more positive mark on the metal.

- Next, mark and cut the last metal. Doing this is essential if you need to finish the curve professionally.

- Secure your decking by drilling hex head screws into pre-drilled holes.

- Using Plas Pro fascia supports to support the joists correctly because the design incorporates a curve.

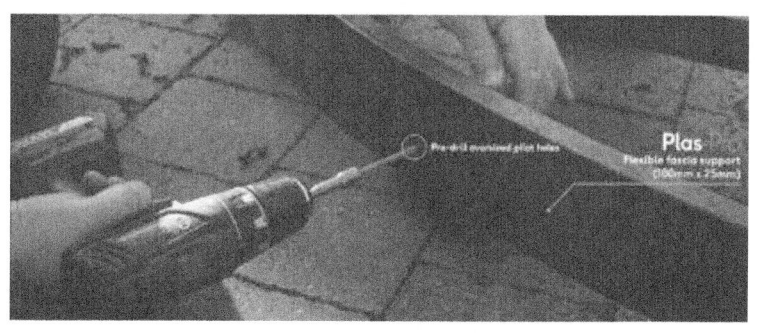

- Next, fix and trim the decking boards. Cut the boards into the required measurements, then support them with joists.

- At this point, you will notice that the ends are not neat. Do not worry about this; the boards should overhang the Plasmbro support.

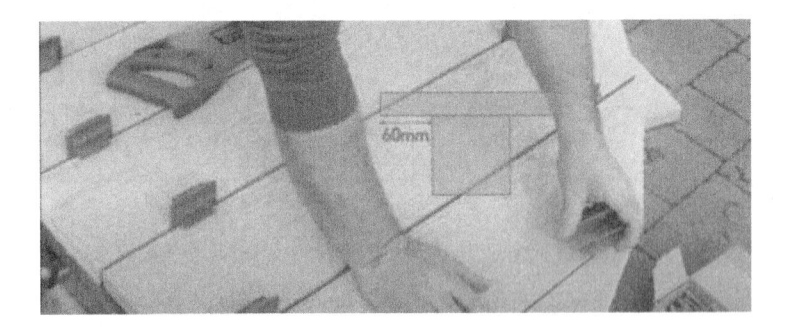

- Next, mark a line on the boards. This will show where to cut the boards to follow the curve.

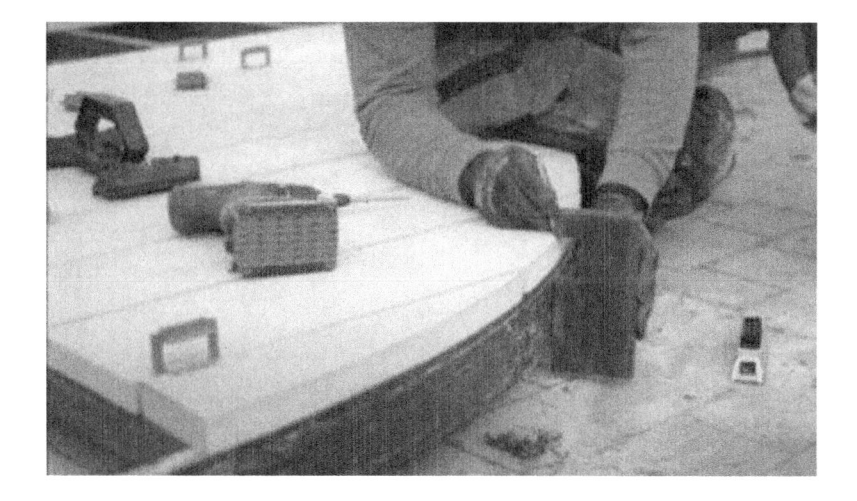

- Next, cut off the areas that are past the marked areas.

- Next, use sandpaper to smoothen the edges

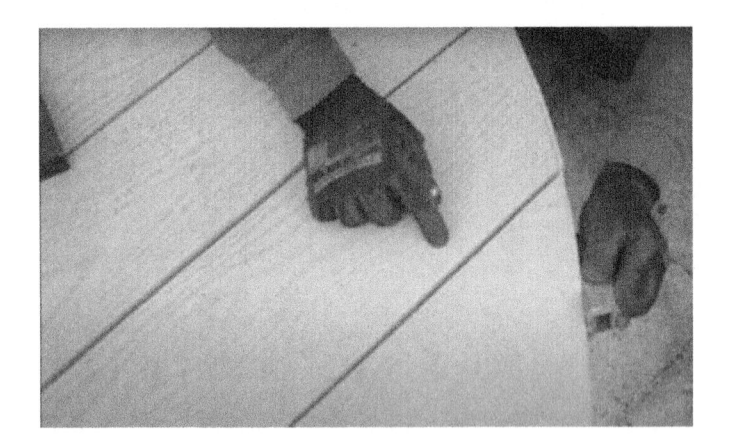

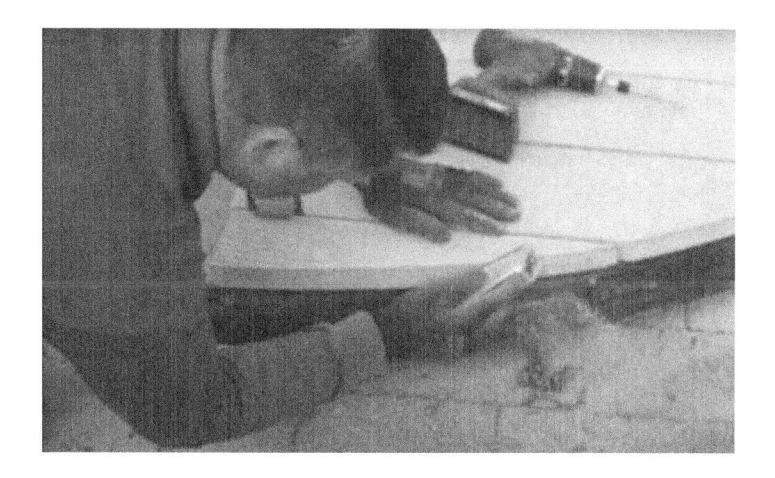

- Next, add another layer of Plas Pro fascia for additional support.

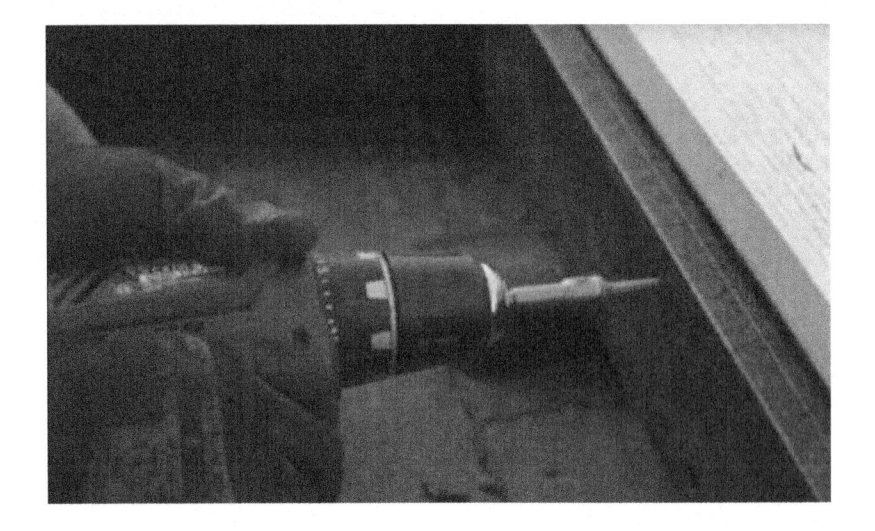

- Apply millboard touch-up coating to any visible cuts.

- Next, add edging and fascia to the curve.

Deck Building Made Easy for Beginners

- Next, smoothen the fascia.

- Next, add glue to the edges.

- Cover that space with a second Plasma facial support

- Screw the additional fascia in a diagonal motion

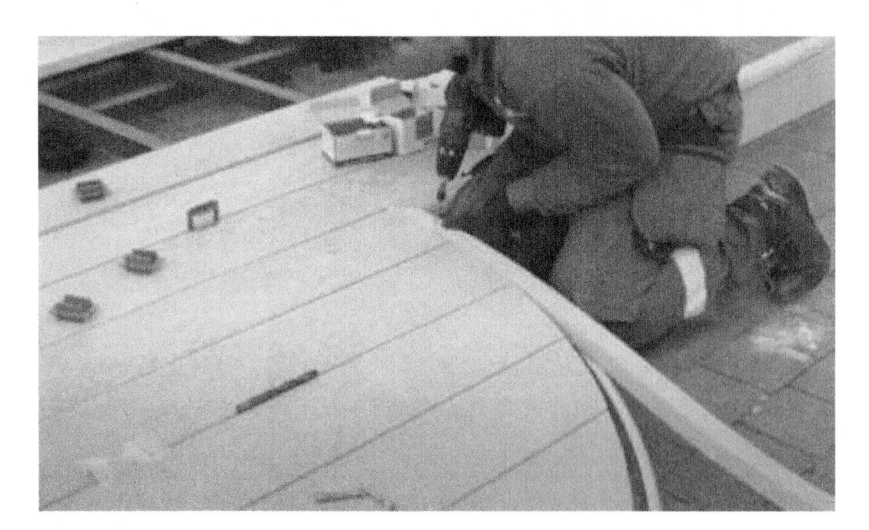

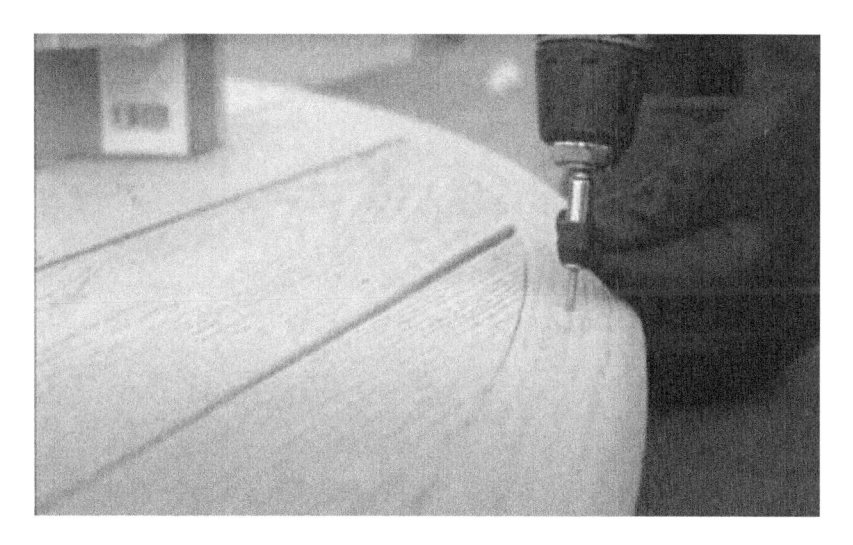

And you are done!

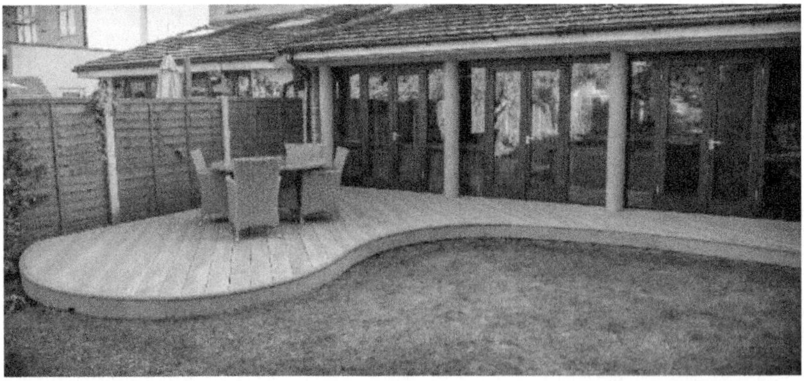

Deck 7: A Floating Deck on A Sloping Yard

Materials Required

- Spray
- Sod cutter

- Carpenter's level
- Tamper
- Tuffblock
- Brush
- Lumber
- Sealant
- Saw
- Drill
- Protective tape

Procedure

- First, prepare the site, then mark out the deck's dimensions using a straight edge.

- Take a sod cutter, set it to three-quarters inch depth, and let it roll.

- Next, scope the loose soil with a shovel.

- Next, compact the ground. Dig a trench wide enough for the compactor to lay in.

- Next, set up the individual Tuffblocks. Use the carpenter's level to affirm they are level.

- After digging the trench, affirm once more that it is level.

- Since we are working on a slanted slope, put some paver base on the trenches.

- Next, take a compactor and compact the paver base.

- Here is how your foundation should look so far

Deck Building Made Easy for Beginners

- Next, take some gravel, put some on the area you will place the tuff block on, then place it on top.

Deck Building Made Easy for Beginners

- Next, mark and cut your joists.

- Now seal the exposed ends of your wood.

- Set up the joists. Remember that we are working with a slope. Therefore, you might need help to ensure the joists are level

- At the end of the slope, measure from the base of the tuff block.

- Next, measure and cut your upright posts.

- Next, make additional cuts to adjust for the height of the joists. To do this, measure the width of the joist and set the saw to that width. This will make that depth of a cut into the post.

- Next, grab a hammer and break down the small cuts.

- Next, get a chisel and level that surface.

- When you set up the posts, the woods will take the following shape. This technique will make the deck floor stronger

- Next, treat the cut wood surface

- Next, set up the posts

- Next, screw the woods together.

- Next, attach the joist hangers to the joists, then screw them together

This is how your setup should look so far:

Deck Building Made Easy for Beginners

- Next, add in the center joists.

- Next, strengthen the overhung lumber. To do this, do some deck blocking.

- Next, protect your joists with protective tape.

- Next, lay your decking boards and screw them together.

- Next, trim off the edges.

- Next, use the excess pieces of wood to make a fascia.

- Next, take more tuff blocks and use them as anchors for the staircase.

- Next, cover the stair skeleton with decking boards.

And you are done

Deck Building Made Easy for Beginners

Deck 8: A Two-Level Pool Deck

Materials Required

- Composite material
- Water shield

- Black aluminum balusters
- Lattice
- Rake
- Crushed Stone
- Wheelbarrow
- Beam tape
- Saw
- Tape measure
- String
- Screws
- Auger
- Concrete mix
- Water
- Thomson's water seal
- Brush

Procedure

- First, clear some parts of the sliding to help you locate where the posts and framing bands will go.

- Next, mark the center of the post, then measure over and set up the layout string.

Deck Building Made Easy for Beginners

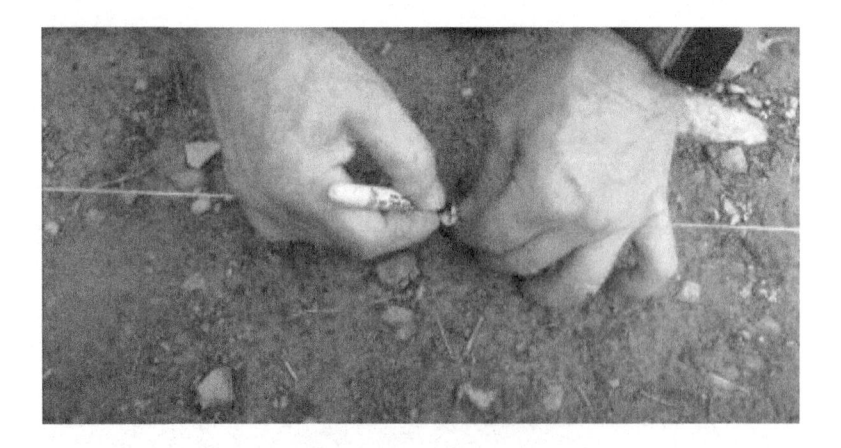

- Mark where the deck posts will go.

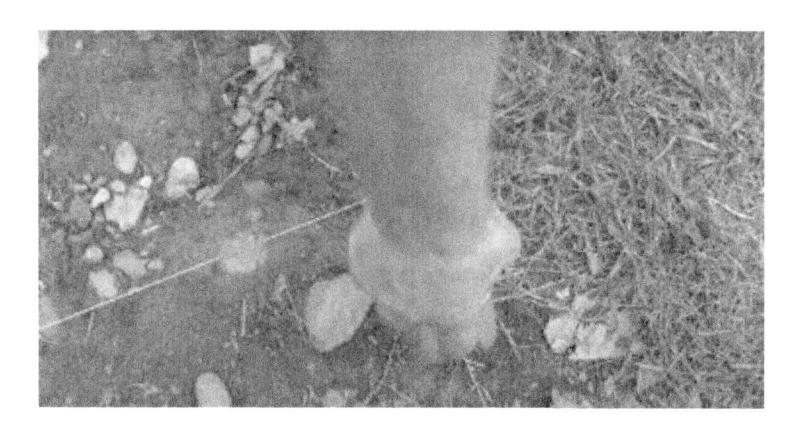

- Drill in the deck holes.

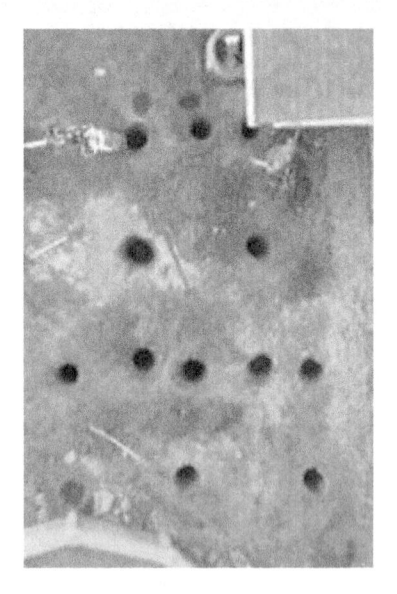

- Next, add concrete.

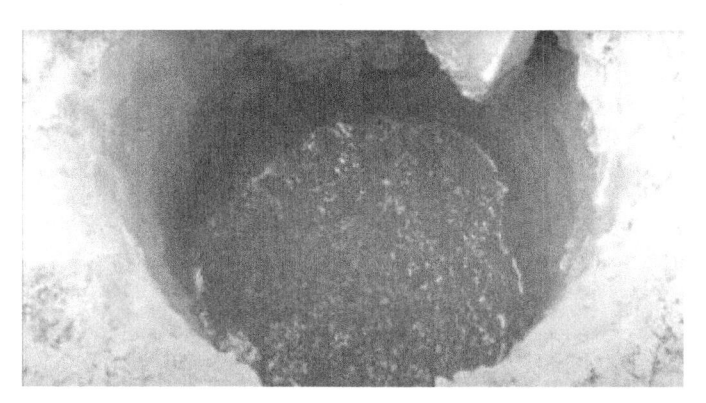

- Next, give your lumber some coating.

- Next, install a water shield to help seal any spaces.

- Next, fit in some lumber to the house. This will help you attach the deck to the house.

- Next, install a metal flashing.

- Next, add another flashing.

- Next, put some flashing on top.

- Next, put flashing on top of the wood.

By now, the sealant we applied to our posts has aired out. So, next, put your poles into the holes.

- Next, attach the poles to the frames.

- Next, trim the excess depending on the height you want for the deck.

- To make the poles stronger, cover them with another board.

- Add in the other joists.

Deck Building Made Easy for Beginners

- Next, work on the center pole.

- For a stronger center, attach two boards, then set it up.

Deck Building Made Easy for Beginners

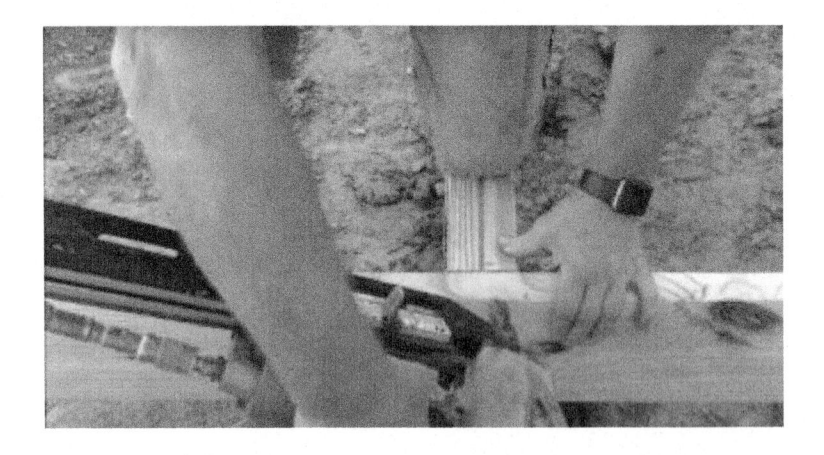

- Next, set up the upper deck.

- Next, trim off the excess.

Deck Building Made Easy for Beginners

- Next, install the two side bands, ensuring they are level

- Next, put the frame around the pool.

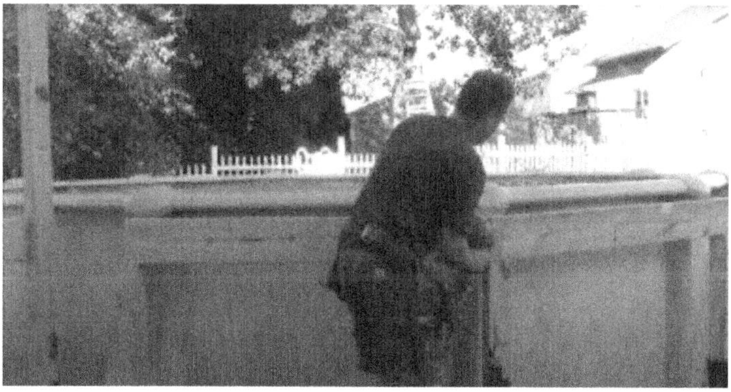

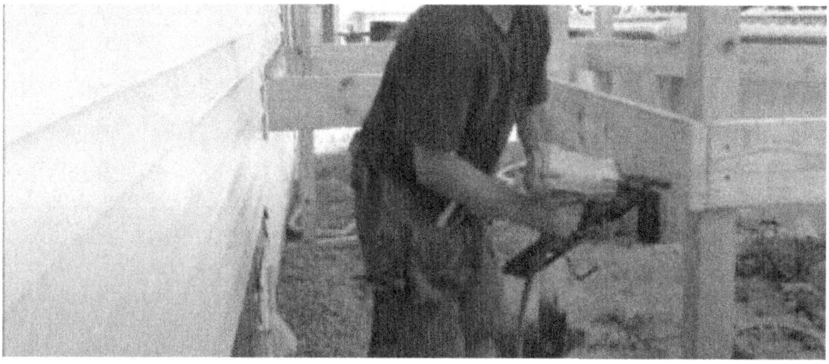

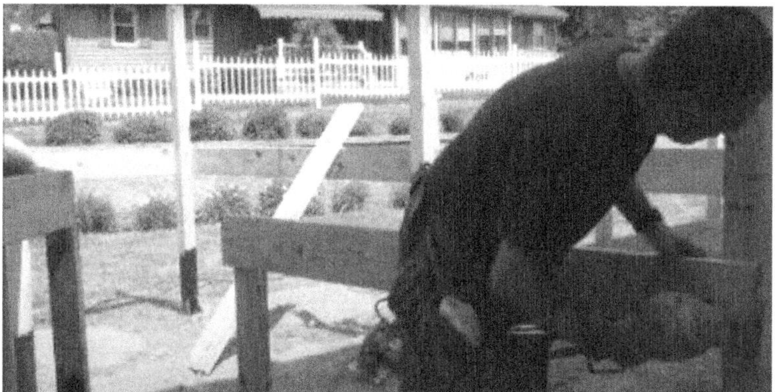

- After fixing a board with another, add hangers for additional support.

- Next, backfill the soil and try to make the ground flat.

- Next, lay down a landscape fabric.

- Next, take the crushed stones and spread them over the landscape fabric.

Deck Building Made Easy for Beginners

- To strengthen the deck, add a board to the front and strengthen it with more joist hangers. Adding this extra board will strengthen the floor joists.

- Next, seal the wood, specifically the posts. I used Thomson's water seal. This sealant will prevent the posts from drying too fast due to the sun.

- Next, measure, cut, and set up the floor joists.

- Next, add the floor joists.

Deck Building Made Easy for Beginners

The image below represents the complete joist installation.

Deck Building Made Easy for Beginners

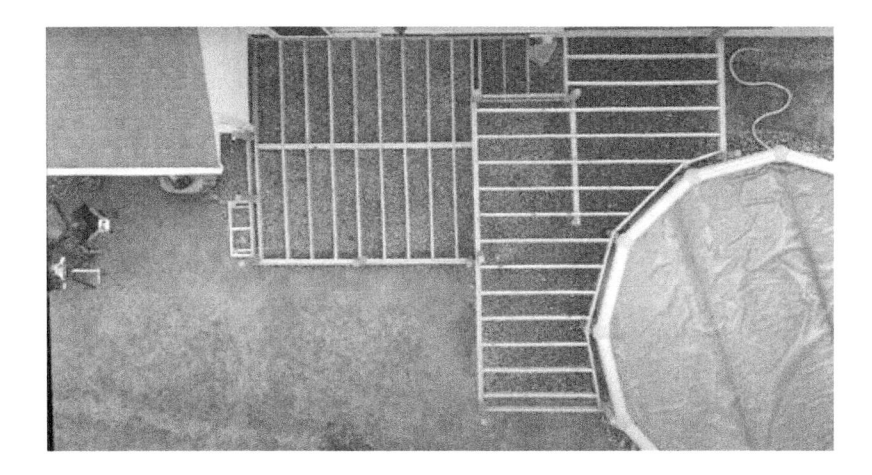

- Next, work on the steps

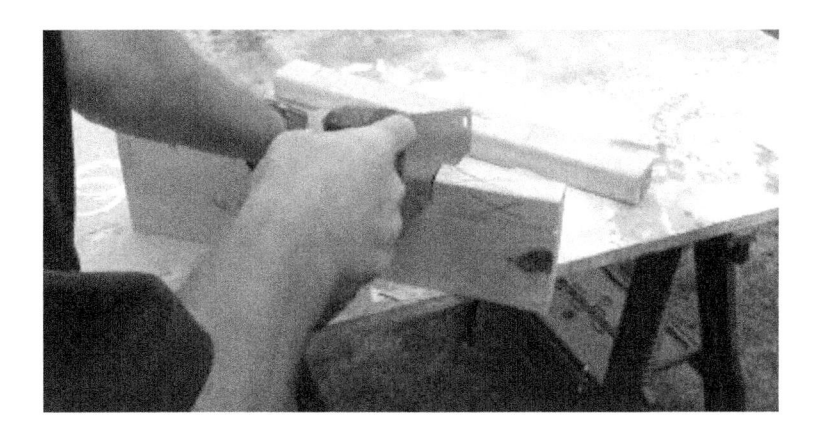

- Ensure the step lumbers are level.

- Next, fix the stair poles.

- To make the step stronger, do more deck blocking.

- Next, backfill the dirt to fill the post holes.

- Next, add more framing to the whole outer frame for more deck strength.

- Next, apply your tape all over the frame.

- Install some boards below to get ample space between the top and bottom ground boards.

- Next, add joy deck ties to the joint area.

- Next, measure, mark and cut the fascia board. Then, fix the fascia board to the deck.

- Add Cortex hidden fasteners on top of the normal screws for a more professional look.

Deck Building Made Easy for Beginners

- Next, install a custom-painted carriage

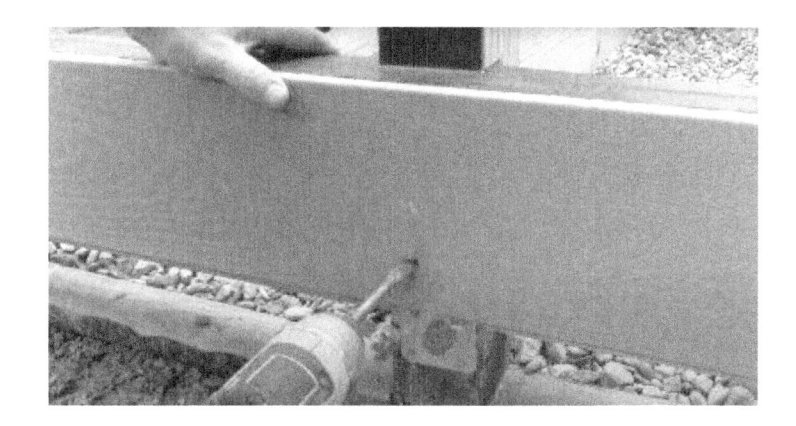

Deck Building Made Easy for Beginners

- Next, add your decking.

- Remember to put spacers in the middle of the decking boards.

Deck Building Made Easy for Beginners

- Add some deck spacers to the bottom of the deck. I decided on this to give my deck a more professional finish. Do not screw them tightly together – this prevents proper circulation.

- If you get to a spot with a screw, curve out the scrap, make a hole, and finally fit in the scrap. No one will know that there is a screw underneath.

Deck Building Made Easy for Beginners

Deck Building Made Easy for Beginners

- Next, if you had taken off a huge part of the house's sliding, refix it since the floor is already complete.

- Next, install your railing system. To do this, measure and cut it into the size you want, then slide it over the wooden post.

- Next, attach the post-sleeve cap and post-sleeve skirt

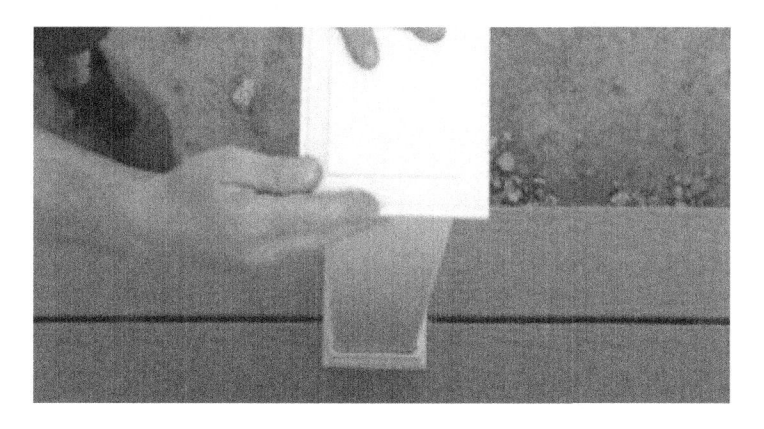

Deck Building Made Easy for Beginners

Page | 339

- Next, pick out your top and bottom railing parts, baluster, and infill kit and assemble it.

- Start by fixing the top bracket.

- Next, fix the bottom bracket.

- Next, affix the railings.

- Next, affix the balusters.

- Trex railings come as a whole kit. The last thing you should do is affix the closures.

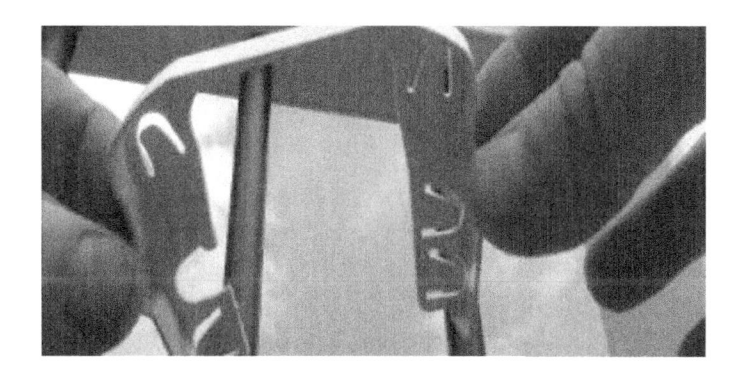

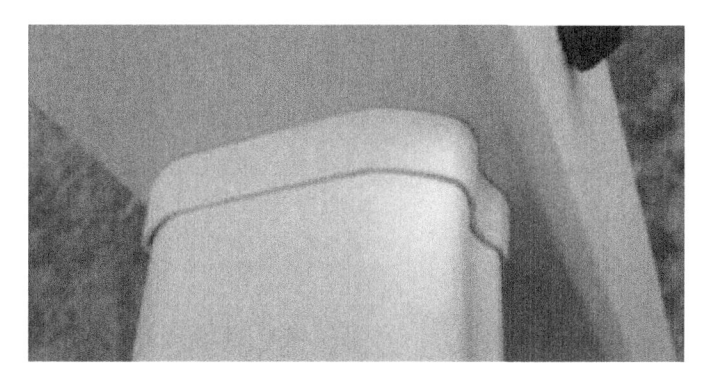

Deck Building Made Easy for Beginners

Page | 343

Deck Building Made Easy for Beginners

- Next, add in the lattice.

Page | 344

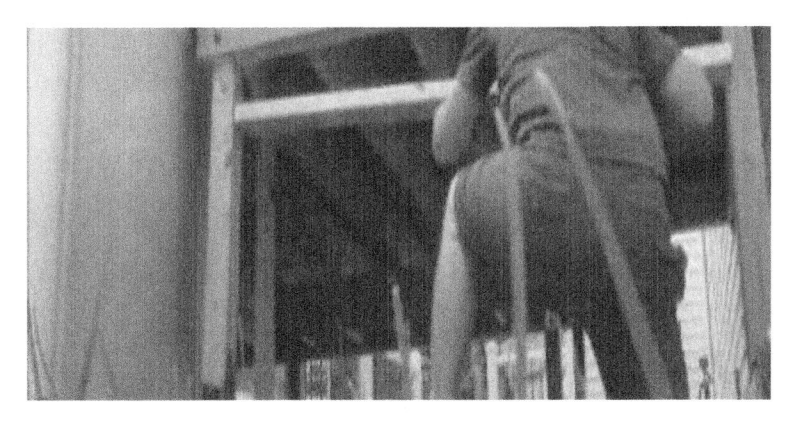

- To protect the wood from rot, apply a sealant.

- Next, measure, cut, and install the lattice.

You can leave the lattice as full as it is, or make that space useable by making a door. If you would like to make a door, follow the steps below;

- Make a square from metal.

Deck Building Made Easy for Beginners

Deck Building Made Easy for Beginners

- Next, make the other stair to the upper deck
- Start by making the stringers

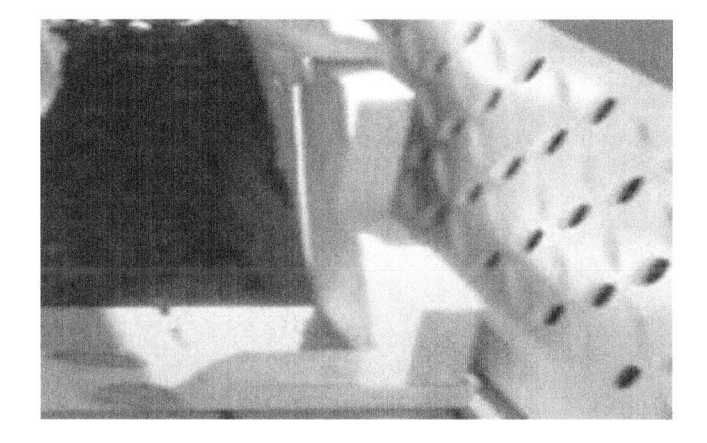

- Next, put some tape on top of the stringers.

- Next, add on the fascia boards, then cover them with more decking.

Deck Building Made Easy for Beginners

- Finally, make your entrance. Cut the door and melt the metal pieces together depending on your desired door shape.

Deck Building Made Easy for Beginners

Deck 9: Front Yard Deck

Materials Required

- Spray
- Hammer
- Hurdles
- String line
- Water
- Hoop wine
- Wheelbarrow
- Shovel
- Carpenter's level

- Chalk/pencil

- Saw

- Ruler

- Nails

- Nail gun

For this project, kindly note that I am working with two surfaces (existing concrete and soil), as seen below;

Procedure

- First, map out where the deck will be

- Next, position your hurdles. Do the positioning away from the deck to allow you enough working room

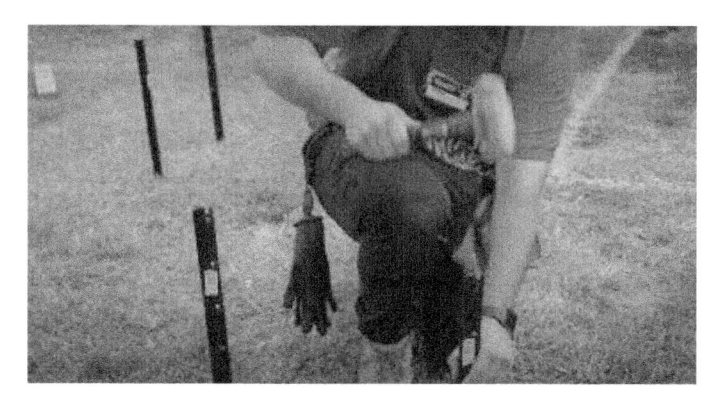

For safety precautions, use post caps

- Next, screw timber onto the hurdles. You will use the hurdles to secure the string line.

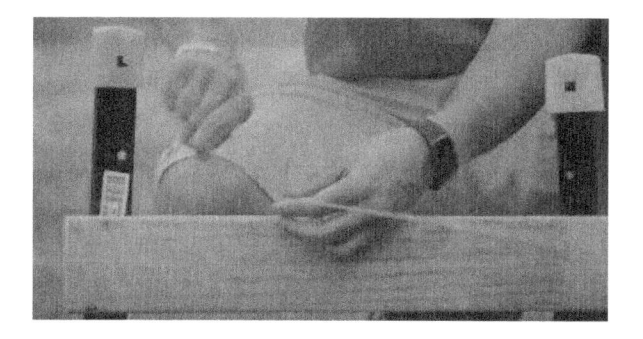

- Next, install stamps.

- To do this, first, dig out and remove some soil.

- Next, identify the stump and bearer positions.

- Next, dig the holes. The post holes should be at least 100 millimeters; 600 millimeters will suffice.

- Apply a coat of bitumen paint.

- While the bitumen paint is drying, go ahead and mix the concrete.

- Next, put the concrete into the post holes.

- Next, put the stumps into the hole.

- Use a carpenter's level to ensure that the stamps level.

- Next, backfill the holes with soil, then let it dry overnight.

- Next, mark the stumps at the bottom of the barrier and cut them.

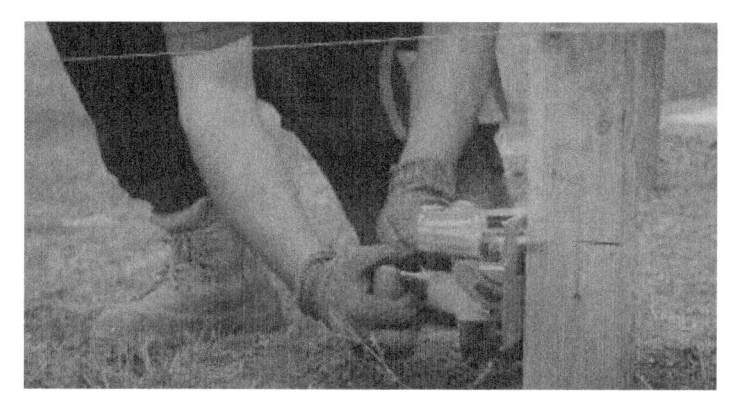

- To get the length of the bearer, measure the distance from the house to the string line.

- Using these measurements, cut the lumber.

- Next, laminate the two pieces of timber together to increase the strength of the wood.

- Tie the jointed wood using a hoop wine

- Next, nail both sides of the bearer to the posts

- Next, take your tin snips and cut off the excess hoop iron

- Next, add a waving plate against the wall

- Next, put in the joists

For that much-needed rigidity, add noggings

- In addition to adding the noggings after every two joists, add brackets.

- For further support, place adjustable feet under the joists. Do this in every concentrated area.

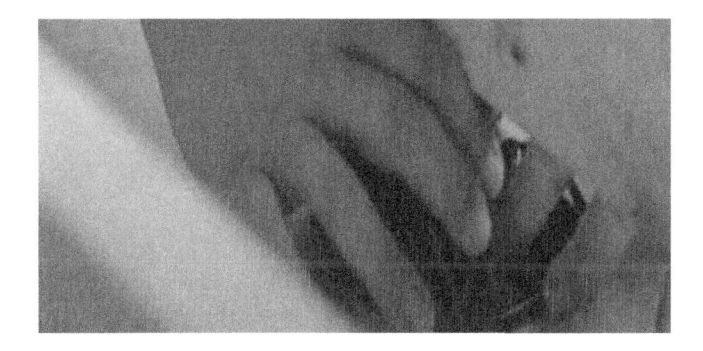

- Next, measure and mark where the stumps will go. This will make the deck's step stronger.

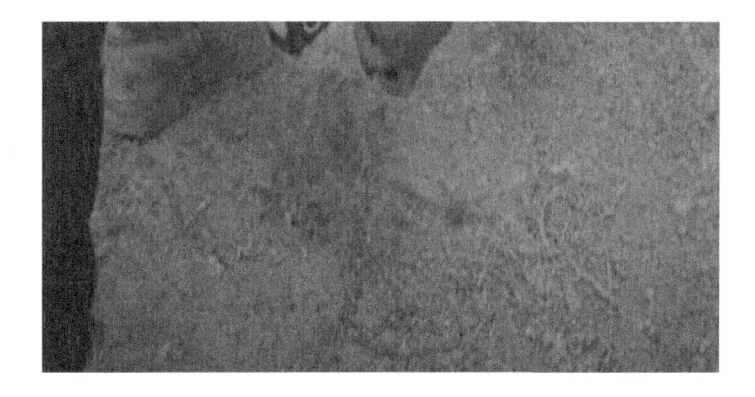

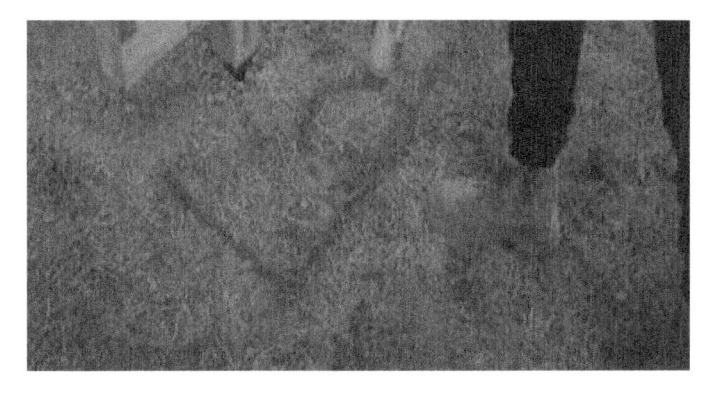

- Next, dig the holes for the stumps.

- Next, measure and cut your staircase steps.

- Before putting these posts in, apply a coat of bitumen paint as we did before to ensure the timber does not rot.

- Next, mix concrete and pour it into the staircase holes.

- Ensure these poles are level.

- Next, backfill the holes.

- To work out the height of the staircase step, measure the height from the top of the joists to the ground. Next, divide the result you get by two, then subtract the height of the subfloor. This will give you the height of the stump. Even as you do these calculations, keep in mind that the minimum height of a single step is 140, and the maximum should be 190.

- With your height in mind, cut the posts.

- Next, measure and mark the depth and thickness of the lumber.

- Next, saw to the thickness of the timber.

- Next, take a chisel and level out the cut-off part.

- Next, do not forget to keep the joist spacing the same by setting your outside beam up on the deck and then marking the existing joists.

Deck Building Made Easy for Beginners

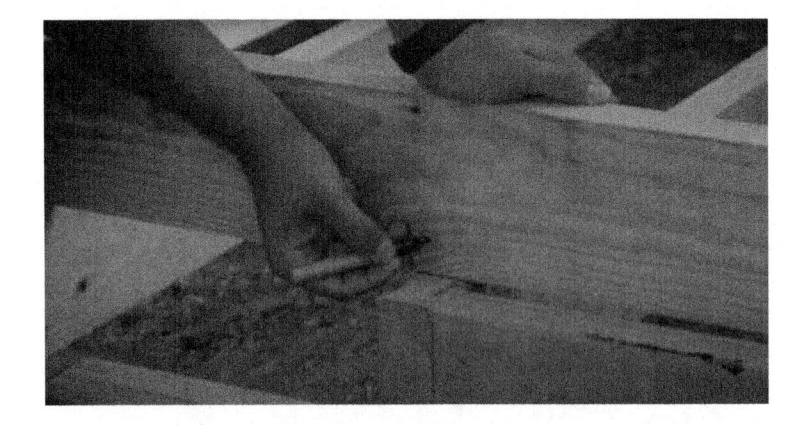

- Next, build a subfloor.

- To complete the subfloor, screw it into place. Just ensure you keep checking for levelness.

- For further support, screw in joist hangers.

- Next, lay down the deck boards. The easiest way to do this is to place every fifth board down first. In addition, use your pre-drawn marks for accuracy.

- Next, pre-drill because you do not want to splint the timber when you begin drilling.

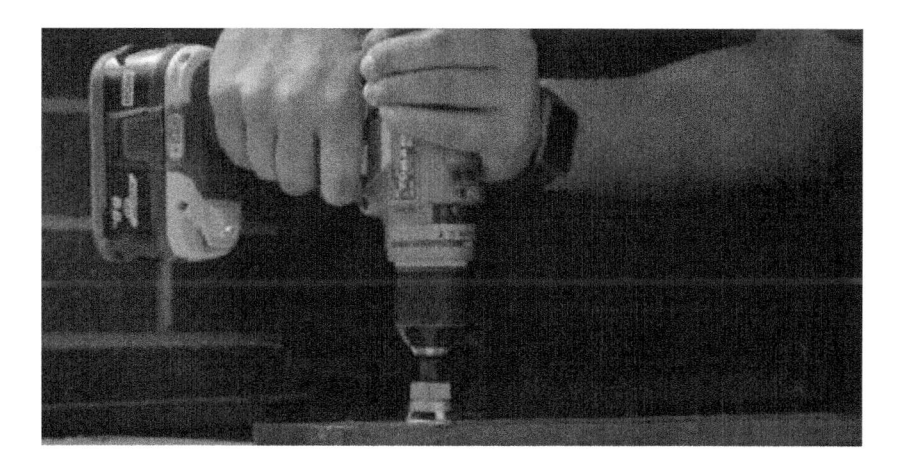

You will grab some screws and use them to drill into the wood. Always stagger your lumber joints and ensure they occur on top of the joists. In addition, remember to leave some additional length overhanging on the board so that it becomes easy to cut after completing a step.

To ensure the nailing or screwing is in line –use carpenter's chalk. As you install the boards, put wedges in between every board. All you will be doing is pre-drill and screw.

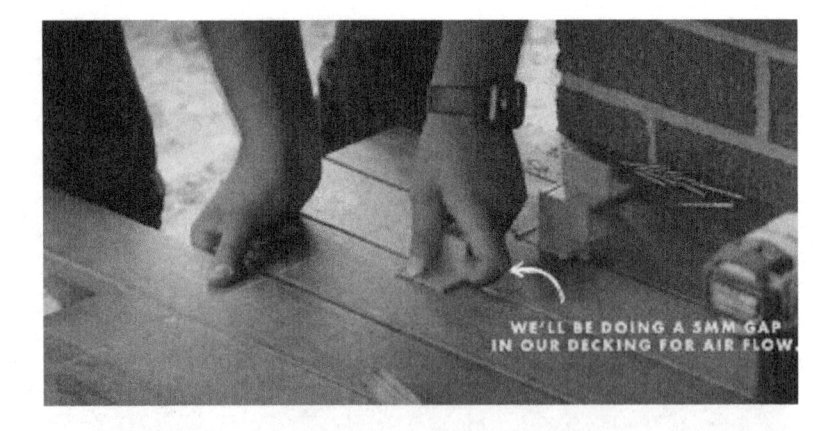

Wedges are important because they help with spacing the deck boards evenly.

- Next, take a circular saw and the excess decking boards off.

Next, attach your screening from the top to the bottom.

- Next, do not forget to lay decking on the steps.

It looks beautiful so far, right?

What if you have a tree in your back or front yard and would like to have a deck without uprooting the tree? Then the next design is your ideal choice.

Deck 10: A Deck Around the Pool

Deck Building Made Easy for Beginners

Materials Required

- Drill
- Water
- Concrete
- Lumber
- Shovel
- Sandpaper
- Lumber
- Screws

- Hinges
- Lattice
- Latches
- Hammer

Procedure

- Dig 11 holes or the number of holes you will require to support the deck. Each hole should be around 3 feet.

- Next, pour concrete into the hole.

- Then, pour some water into the hole.

- Next, mix the two, then fix the post.

- Then attach a frame around the pool.

- Then, fix the frame.

- Then, ensure that the timber is level.

- Continue framing the deck.

Deck Building Made Easy for Beginners

- With the posts ready, trim off the edges according to the measurement of the deck. After trimming the posts, backfill the posts.

- Next, frame the pool area.

Deck Building Made Easy for Beginners

- Next, measure, cut, and screw/nail in your joists

Page | 396

- Next, measure the railing posts from the main pole, then trim the excess wood.

Deck Building Made Easy for Beginners

Here is how your skeleton should look so far

- Since we need this deck to be stronger, add more framing to the bottom post sections.

- Next, add in a lattice to close off the bottom part.

- Next, put a frame on the edges of the lattice. This will secure the lattice.

- Next, get your lattices, fashion them into a small rectangle, add hinges and make a door.

- Next, work on the staircase. Staircase stringers follow some basic rules discussed for most decks in this book. Let us remind ourselves.

- First, identify where the bottom step of the staircase will be.

A long level on top of the decking will be set. The height will be measured right where the steps will end. For instance, if the height is 55 inches, it will be divided by 7 (this is the recommended height for staircase steps). Take the result you get and round it off to the nearest number; you will get 8. These will be the raisers we will be working towards.

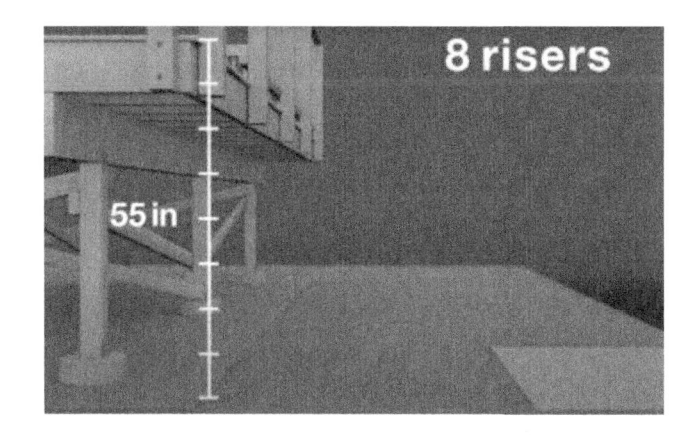

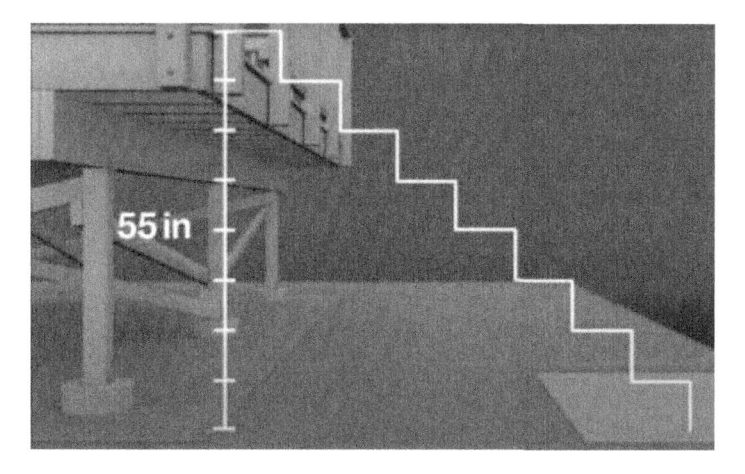

To determine the measurements of each step, divide the original height by the number of raisers.

With this in mind, let us get back to building the deck.

- Measure and cut your stringers.

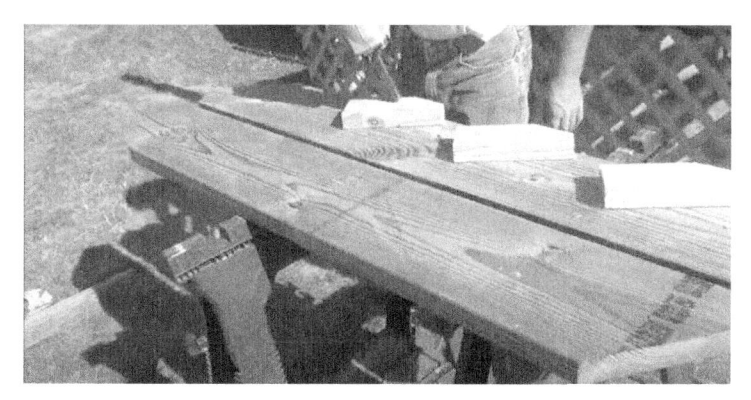

Deck Building Made Easy for Beginners

- Next, to strengthen the staircase, add a frame at the bottom and screw it to the staircase.

- Next, add the next of the staircase steps.

- Next, work on the railings. To do this, dig a hole and put in poles.

- Next, screw these poles to the staircase step. While doing the screwing, use your carpenter's level to ensure they are straight.

- Next, measure the edges of the railing posts and trim them according to your measurements.

- Next, measure the staircase boards (this one will join the posts you have just done to the deck), seal with a sealant, then screw them to the deck.

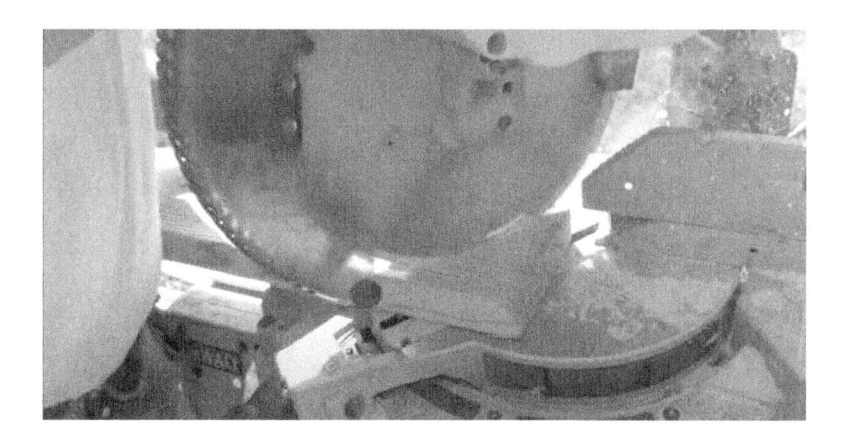

Deck Building Made Easy for Beginners

- Next, measure, cut, and screw in your decking boards.

- Next, trim off the edges using a circular saw.

This should be the progress of your deck so far

Next, get your pieces of wood and make your railings

For easy screwing of the railings, lay them down in a straight line, make a line with a straight edge and pre-drill the holes

- Next, apply a sealant to these pieces of railings

- Once these railings dry off, screw them to two horizontal boards as shown below

- Next, slide it down the railing posts and screw them

- Next, add a door to the deck –this is optional. All you need to do is take the railings, screw them to two horizontal boards, then take one diagonal board and screw it on top of the door.

- Next, add a latch to the door

- Next, screw in safety boards on top of the decking rails

Finally, for a smoother touch, take your sandpaper and sand these safety boards

And you are done!

Deck Building Made Easy for Beginners

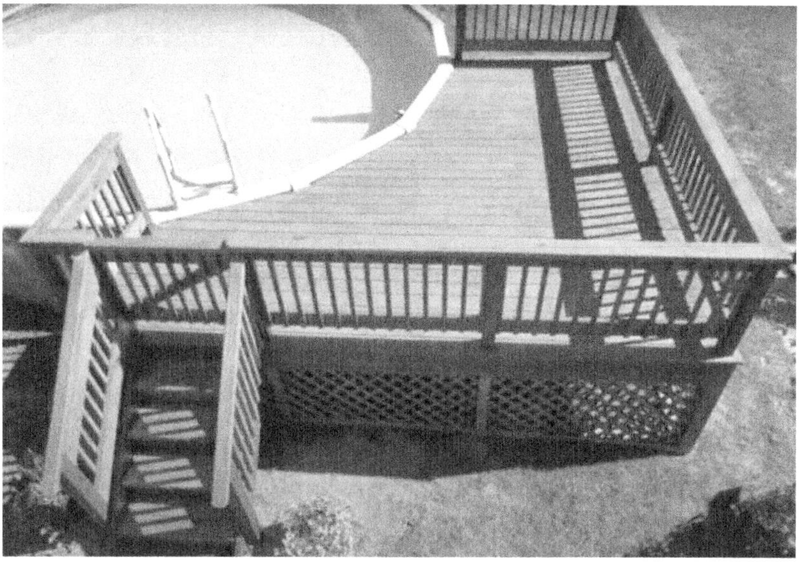

Chapter 6: Deck Maintenance and Repair

This final chapter outlines essential deck maintenance and repair tips that can make all the difference:

Clean the Deck

Cleaning your deck might not seem so important during the cold winter months, but the truth is that cleaning is an all-year job. Thorough cleaning will prevent slippy situations, a common complication that happens during winter.

Additionally:

Cleaning will prevent mildew and stains and will allow you to identify wobbly rails, loose boards, nails, and screws that may otherwise cause safety issues if left unattended.

Clean your deck at least once every year. In addition, your deck needs an annual exfoliation to give protective sealers time to seep deeper and deeper into the wood.

For a thorough clean, you will need the following materials;

- **Deck cleaner.** You can choose one of the following;

    o **Borax:** This cleaner has an ingredient called borate, an all-purpose natural cleaner. Use a ratio of one cup for every gallon of water.

    o **Oxygen bleach cleaner:** Unlike normal bleach, oxygen bleach cleaners are safer for the environment. They are not powerful when dealing with stubborn algae or mold but using them regularly will help get the desired result. When using this cleaner, protect yourself using gloves and goggles.

    o **Spray-and-Forget-it products:** Such products are many, and their ingredients vary. However, they all work towards removing stains such as mildew, moss, and mold, among others. A few of these products include Wet & Forget, Spray & Forget, Moldex by EnviroCare, and Bayer 2-in-1 Moss & Algae Killer, among others

- Safety glasses

- Mask

- Measuring bowl or cup

- Pressure washer

- Gloves

- Brooms

With these tools in hand, follow the steps below to clean your deck;

- First, sweep. You can use a soft broom to remove dirt or leaves, and a strong bristled brush and water for a thorough clean.

- Next, get a high-pressure cleaner and clean the whole deck as carefully as possible. Use a hose if you cannot get your hands on a high-pressure cleaner.

- Next, scrub the deck. Depending on your cleaner of choice, mix the deck cleaner with some water, dip the deck scrub broom into the mixture, then scrub the deck. Before you begin cleaning, give the mixture approximately 20 minutes. In addition, take care not to get the cleaning mix on the plants.

Finally, after scrubbing it carefully, wash the deck down with a hose or a high-pressure cleaner, then leave it to dry. And your deck is clean!

Seal the deck

After a clean, I recommend sealing the deck. Here is why:

A wooden surface requires a proper sealant to protect it from the ravaging sun and the effects of rain and temperature fluctuations. Before you follow the steps below, kindly note that you should not apply sealants in direct sunlight. This is because the finish will dry too quickly. If you used treated wood to build your deck, do not apply a sealant until four weeks pass. Why four weeks? Well, by this time, the wood will have completely dried.

With this in mind, let us get to sealing the deck!

- First, plan when to apply the sealant. I recommend doing it when it is not rainy because you will need at least two days of dry weather to get the best seal.

- Next, sand your deck. This helps ensure that the sealant penetrates the wood. Remember to do the sanding in the direction of the grain. If you have a big deck, use a pole or palm sander to speed up the process.

- Next, apply your sealer. However, do not shake or stir the sealant because this may cause bubbles to form in the finish. Use a paint roller, brush, or sprayer to apply the sealant. Apply a thin coat, but you can always add another later (thin coats penetrate the wood better than thick coats).

- Finally, allow the deck to dry completely before using it. Drying time ranges between 24 and 72 hours.

Stain your deck

Your deck may fade after a while. When it does, instead of re-building it, you can stain it. Staining will bring out its rich original color and texture while at the same time protecting it from any harsh elements and keeping the wood from warping.

Staining may require more time and energy, but the truth is that doing it will lead to minimal work in the future.

To stain your deck, follow the steps below;

- Go around your deck and look for imperfections such as broken screws or nails, warped wood, broken wood, and nails raised above the deck's surface, among others.

- Next, clean the deck.

- After the deck dries up, stain it. If you do not want to stain some parts, block them using a standard painter's tape. In addition, cover any vegetation close to the deck as the stain may damage it.

  To apply the stain, use a roller brush and aim for a steady coat. If you notice an area with too much stain, use the roller brush to fix the imperfections.

- Finally, allow the deck to dry. This will take between 24 and 48 hours, depending on the wood your used to build the deck and the temperature and humidity.

Repair your deck

Repairing your deck may not always be necessary because decks can stand the test of time. However, I urge you to inspect your deck to find out if you need to repair it. You need to look for the following;

- Broken wood

- Splintered wood
- Corroded metal
- Rotten spots
- Loose nails
- Unsecured railings

When you notice any spot that requires repair, gather your tools. Always have the following tools ready;

- Sander
- Drill
- Saw
- Shovel
- Tape measure

Replace any cracked, broken, or damaged boards. To do this, carefully remove the nails and then the damaged planks. As you do this, be keen not to harm adjacent planks. Once you complete doing your repairs, seal and stain the wood.

Use the following checklist to help you go through your deck;

Item	Checked
Ledger board	
Joists	
Support posts	
Deck boards	
Ledger boards	
Stairs	
Railings	
Stair risers	
Stringers	
Stray nails	
Loose screws	
Rusted Fasteners	
Rusted screws and nails	

Conclusion

As this guide has affirmed, deck building is not a pro affair alone. It is not an activity or art secluded for professionals with years of experience. Building a deck is something you can do. All you have to do is BEGIN.

Good luck

PS: I'd like your feedback. If you are happy with this book, please leave a review on Amazon.

Please leave a review for this book on Amazon by visiting the page below:

https://amzn.to/2VMR5qr

Printed in Great Britain
by Amazon